CAMBRIDGE LIBRARY COLLECTION

Books of enduring scholarly value

Religion

For centuries, scripture and theology were the focus of prodigious amounts of scholarship and publishing, dominated in the English-speaking world by the work of Protestant Christians. Enlightenment philosophy and science, anthropology, ethnology and the colonial experience all brought new perspectives, lively debates and heated controversies to the study of religion and its role in the world, many of which continue to this day. This series explores the editing and interpretation of religious texts, the history of religious ideas and institutions, and not least the encounter between religion and science.

Catalogue of the Syriac MSS. in the Convent of S. Catharine on Mount Sinai

The sisters Agnes Lewis (1843–1926) and Margaret Gibson (1843–1920) were pioneering biblical scholars who became experts in a number of ancient languages. Travelling widely in the Middle East, they made several significant discoveries, including one of the earliest manuscripts of the Four Gospels in Syriac, a dialect of Aramaic, the language probably spoken by Jesus himself. Their chief discoveries were made in the Monastery of St. Catherine on Mount Sinai. This work is a list of the monastery's manuscripts in Syriac, compiled by Agnes Lewis in 1893 and first published in 1894. Written in English and Modern Greek for use as a tool for scholars and for the monks themselves, this fascicule provides a careful document of the monastery's Syriac pages, their physical state and content. This text will be of great interest to Syriac scholars and those interested in Middle Eastern monastic and broader Christian history.

T0364262

Cambridge University Press has long been a pioneer in the reissuing of out-of-print titles from its own backlist, producing digital reprints of books that are still sought after by scholars and students but could not be reprinted economically using traditional technology. The Cambridge Library Collection extends this activity to a wider range of books which are still of importance to researchers and professionals, either for the source material they contain, or as landmarks in the history of their academic discipline.

Drawing from the world-renowned collections in the Cambridge University Library and other partner libraries, and guided by the advice of experts in each subject area, Cambridge University Press is using state-of-the-art scanning machines in its own Printing House to capture the content of each book selected for inclusion. The files are processed to give a consistently clear, crisp image, and the books finished to the high quality standard for which the Press is recognised around the world. The latest print-on-demand technology ensures that the books will remain available indefinitely, and that orders for single or multiple copies can quickly be supplied.

The Cambridge Library Collection brings back to life books of enduring scholarly value (including out-of-copyright works originally issued by other publishers) across a wide range of disciplines in the humanities and social sciences and in science and technology.

Catalogue of the Syriac MSS. in the Convent of S. Catharine on Mount Sinai

AGNES SMITH LEWIS

CAMBRIDGE UNIVERSITY PRESS

Cambridge, New York, Melbourne, Madrid, Cape Town,
Singapore, São Paolo, Delhi, Mexico City

Published in the United States of America by Cambridge University Press, New York

www.cambridge.org
Information on this title: www.cambridge.org/9781108043519

This edition first published 1894
This digitally printed version 2012

ISBN 978-1-108-04351-9 Paperback

CATALOGUE

OF SYRIAC MSS.

London: C. J. CLAY AND SONS,
CAMBRIDGE UNIVERSITY PRESS WAREHOUSE,
AVE MARIA LANE.
Glasgow: 263, ARGYLE STREET.

Cambridge: DEIGHTON, BELL AND CO.
Leipzig: F. A. BROCKHAUS.
New York: MACMILLAN AND CO.

PLATE I.

III Maccabees I. 8—17
From a Sinaitic MS.

Frontispiece

STUDIA SINAITICA No. I.

CATALOGUE

OF THE SYRIAC MSS.

IN THE CONVENT OF S. CATHARINE ON MOUNT SINAI

COMPILED BY

AGNES SMITH LEWIS.

LONDON:

C. J. CLAY AND SONS,

CAMBRIDGE UNIVERSITY PRESS WAREHOUSE

AVE MARIA LANE.

1894

Cambridge:

PRINTED BY C. J. CLAY, M.A., AND SONS,

AT THE UNIVERSITY PRESS.

τῷ μακαριωτάτῳ καὶ φιλομούσῳ

ΚΥΡΙῼ ΠΟΡΦΥΡΙῼ

Τῷ τοῦ Ὄρους Σινᾶ Ἀρχιερεῖ

ὑπολήψεώς τε καὶ εὐγνωμοσύνης

ἐλάχιστον δεῖγμα

προσφέρει

ἡ συντάκτης

INTRODUCTION.

THE following list of the Syriac manuscripts in the Convent of St Catherine on Mount Sinai was made by me in the month of February, 1893. It is not a complete catalogue of their contents, the time at my disposal (forty days) and the necessity of completing other work to which I had set my hands having precluded me from compiling anything that goes much beyond a mere index. I took advantage of an opportunity that has never before been granted to a European visitor, and which sprung directly out of a visit paid by my sister, Mrs Gibson, and myself to the monastery in February, 1892.

I had then the pleasure of discovering and photographing the palimpsest, No. 30, which contains the Four Gospels in Old Syriac, a Palestinian Syriac Lectionary, No. 1, a tenth century Arabic codex of the Gospels, a ninth century Arabic codex of some of St Paul's Epistles, and a Greek Liturgy of St Mark of Alexandria; some of these being hitherto unknown in Europe, and others being known by one, or in the case of the Liturgy, by two copies only.

My sister and I had also gained the goodwill of His Beatitude Porphyrios, Archbishop of Mount Sinai, and of the whole resident community of monks, from whom we received an amount of kindness and assistance which contributed not a little to the success of our efforts. It was thus only natural that my sister should have taken advantage of this friendship to obtain from the Archbishop the following letter, the promise of which, strangely enough, came to us both as a birthday present.

Ὁσιώτατοι Σκευοφύλαξ Κ. Γαλακτίων καὶ Οἰκονόμε Κ. Νικόδημε. Τὴν Ὑμετέραν Ὁσιότητα πατρικῶς εὐχόμεθα καὶ εὐλογοῦμεν.

Αἱ ἐπιδότιδες τῆς συστατικῆς ἡμῶν ταύτης πατρικο-ευχετικῆς ἐπιστολῆς τυγχάνουν, αἱ καὶ πέρυσι συναναβάσαι ἐν τῇ Μονῇ γνωσταὶ ὑμῖν Περιηγήτριαι Ἀδελφαὶ Ἀγγλίδες Κ. Ἄννα Σμὶθ καὶ Μαργαρίτα Γνίβσον, συνοδευόμεναι ὑπὸ τῶν Κ. Κ. Βένσλε μετὰ τῆς συζύγου του, Βάρκερ (sic) μετὰ τῆς συζύγου του, καὶ τοῦ Κυρίου Χάρις, αἵτινες ἔρχονται αὐτόσε πρὸς μελέτην τῆς βιβλιοθήκης τῆς Ἱερᾶς ἡμῶν Μονῆς καὶ πρὸς κατάστρωσιν ἀκριβοῦς καταλόγου ἁπάντων τῶν ἐν αὐτῇ Ἀραβικῶν καὶ Συριακῶν βιβλίων, ὁ ὁποῖος κατάλογος θὰ μένῃ πάντοτε ἐν τῇ Μονῇ ὡς συνενοήθημεν ἐνταῦθα· καὶ μόνον πιστὸν αὐτοῦ ἀντίγραφον θὰ λάβωσιν αἱ ἐν λόγῳ Κυρίαι μεθ᾽ ἑαυτῶν. Ἐπὶ τούτῳ θὰ ἐζήτησαν παρ᾽ ἡμῖν τὴν ἄδειαν τοῦ παραμεῖναι ἕνα περίπου μῆνα αὐτόθι καὶ προτρεπόμεθα ὑμᾶς πατρικῶς ἵνα παράσχητε προθύμως ταῖς ἐριτίμοις καὶ λογίαις ταύταις κυρίαις τὴν πρὸς τὸν σκοπὸν αὐτῶν ἀπαιτουμένην συνδρομὴν καὶ περιποίησιν. Ἐφ᾽ οἷς ἐπευλογοῦντες καὶ αὖθις ὑμᾶς πατρικῶς διατε-λοῦμεν.

τῆς Ὑμετέρας Ὁσιότητος
διάπυρος πρὸς θεὸν εὐχέτης
Ὁ Σιναῖος Πορφύριος.

ἐν Καΐρῳ τῇ 13 Ἰανουαρίου,
1893.

Τοῖς Ὁσιωτάτοις Σκευοφύλαξι Κ. Γαλακτίωνι καὶ Οἰκο-νόμῳ Κ. Νικοδήμῳ τοῖς συγκρατοῦσι τὴν Ἱερὰν τῶν Πατέρων Σύναξιν.

I would draw attention to the conditions under which we obtained permission to examine *all* the Syriac and Arabic books in the Convent. The most important was that a list of these should be made out in the Greek language, and should be left in the Convent, we taking an accurate copy with us on our departure. On the fulfilment of this obligation depended other concessions made to us and to our fellow-travellers, which need not be specified here.

This book is therefore bilingual throughout, the descriptive part being in English and in Modern Greek. In writing the latter I have adopted the ancient forms of the verb εἰμι, such as ἐστι, εἰσι, in preference to εἰνε, so as to make it more readily understood by Western scholars. I have however conformed to modern usage by giving to neuter plural substantives a plural verb.

The work of compiling this list during our stay at the Convent was a heavy one, and I could not have accomplished it but for the constant advice and active assistance of my friend Mr J. Rendel Harris. He alone is responsible for the Appendix of Fragments which he catalogued at the request of the late lamented Abbot and Librarian, Father Galaktion. The text of most of them will be found in his Biblical Fragments from Mount Sinai, published in 1890. No. 55 is the only one of these which I have copied from photographs.

To Mr Harris also I owe the Syriac extracts from No. 10 and No. 16. These he copied from photographs which he took in 1889 and compared again with the originals in 1893.

The dates which I have ventured to assign to some of the MSS. are only approximate, and I suspect that a few of these will be referred to an earlier period when they come into the hands of more experienced scholars.

Certain numbers in my list are left blank; the manuscripts to which these belong having apparently been lost or removed. Mr Harris informs me that one of the missing copies is a fine codex of the second and third books of the Maccabees, which he saw and photographed in 1889.*

I have to record my thanks to the holy Fathers who sometimes relieved me of the task of counting pages; to the Rev. R. H. Kennett of Queens' College, Lecturer in Aramaic to the University of Cambridge, who has helped me with various suggestions in regard to the Syriac extracts; and to Mr J. F. Stenning of Oxford, who has brought me from Sinai some words which I had photographed too faintly in No. 10. And I trust that future visitors to the Sinai Library will forgive any sins of omission which they may detect in these pages, for the sake of the time and labour which may be saved to them in their researches.

* See frontispiece.

AGNES SMITH LEWIS.

CASTLE-BRAE, CAMBRIDGE,
1894.

CONTENTS.

ILLUSTRATIONS.

CORRIGENDA.

Page 17, No. 14 *for* ܩܘܠܝܘܣ *read* ܩܘܠܝܘܣ

Page 50, No. 48 *for* Στιχεράριον *read* Στιχηράριον

Page 51, No. 50 *for* ,, *read* ,,

Page 63, No. 118 *for* ,, *read* ,,

Page 66, No. 133 *for* ,, *read* ,,

Page 69, No. 148 *for* ,, *read* ,,

PLATE II.

Peshito Gospels. No. 2. Sixth century.

LUKE XII. 20—30.

A CATALOGUE
OF SYRIAC MSS. ON MT SINAI

1

Συναξάριον περιέχον τὰ Εὐαγγέλια κατὰ τὴν τάξιν τῶν
Ἑλλήνων. μεμβράνη· ἑκατοστόμετρα κα΄ × ιδ΄· φύλλα σλ΄·
γραμμαὶ ιζ΄· τοῦ ἔτους ͵αρκη΄·

Ἄρχεται·

[Syriac text — three lines]

Synaxarion or Lectionary containing the Gospels according to the order of the Greeks; vellum; 21 centimetres
by 14; 230 leaves; 17 lines; date A.D. 1128.

2

Τὰ Εὐαγγέλια κατὰ τὴν μετάφρασιν Πεσσίτο· καταρτι-
σμένα κατὰ τὴν ἀρχὴν καὶ τὸ τέλος· μεμβράνη· φύλλα ρξγ΄·
ὧν ιδ΄ χάρτινα· ιβ΄ × θ΄· γραμμαὶ κϛ΄· στρογγύλη γραφή· τοῦ
ἔκτου αἰῶνος·

Τὸ ἀρχαῖον κείμενον ἄρχεται ἀπὸ Ματθαίου ιγ΄· μβ΄.

[Syriac text — one line]

Περιέχει δεκατέσσαρας σελίδας προτιθέντος Συναξαρίου
παλιμψήστας· ὄντος τοῦ ὑποκειμένου μέρους τινὸς τοῦ
Εὐαγγελίου κατὰ Λουκᾶν· μετάφρασιν Πεσσίτο.

The Gospels according to the Peshito version; restored at the beginning and end; vellum; 163 leaves, with 14 on paper; 12 × 9; 26 lines; Estrangelo; sixth century. Fourteen pages of a prefixed Synaxarion are palimpsest, the under text being part of the Gospel of Luke, according to the Peshito version.

3

Αἱ τοῦ Ἁγίου Παύλου Ἐπιστολαὶ κατὰ τὴν μετάφρασιν Πεσσίτο. ὀλίγον ἐλλειπὲς τὴν ἀρχήν· μεμβράνη· κη΄ × κα΄· φύλλα ρ΄· δίστηλον· γραμμαὶ κδ΄· στρογγύλη γραφή.

The Pauline Epistles according to the Peshito version; slightly defective at the beginning; vellum; 28 × 21; 100 leaves; two columns; 24 lines; Estrangelo.

4

Τριῴδιον. μεμβράνη· διὰ χάρτου τετελεσμένον· κβ΄ × ιη΄· φύλλα ρϟη΄· ιη΄ χάρτινα· δίστηλον· γραμμαὶ κβ΄· στρογγύλη γραφή· δωδεκάτου αἰῶνος.

Triodion; vellum, completed by paper; 22 × 18; 198 leaves (18 paper); two columns; 22 lines; Estrangelo; twelfth century.

5

Αἱ τοῦ Ἁγίου Παύλου Ἐπιστολαὶ κατὰ τὴν μετάφρασιν Πεσσίτο. φύλλα ρα΄ ἐκ μεμβράνης. Πρόσθετά εἰσι· Αἱ Πράξεις τῶν Ἀποστόλων καὶ αἱ Καθολικαὶ Ἐπιστολαί. φύλλα οε΄ ἐπὶ χάρτου· κε΄ × κ΄· δίστηλον· γραμμαὶ κδ΄· στρογγύλη γραφή· τοῦ ἔκτου αἰῶνος.

The Pauline Epistles according to the Peshito version; vellum; 101 leaves; supplemented by the Acts of the Apostles and Catholic Epistles on paper, in a much later hand; 75 leaves. Including the Antilegomena, 2 Peter, 2 John, 3 John and Jude; 25 × 20; 176 leaves; 2 columns; 24 lines; Estrangelo; sixth century.

6

Συναξάριον τῶν Εὐαγγελίων. ἐλλειπὲς τὴν ἀρχήν· ἡ πρώτη ἀνάγνωσις ἐκ τοῦ Εὐαγγελίου κατὰ Ἰωάννην· μεμβράνη· κγ΄ × ιη΄· φύλλα ρξζ΄· δίστηλον· γραμμαὶ κβ΄· δωδεκάτου αἰῶνος.

A lectionary of the Gospels; imperfect at the beginning; begins with the Gospel of John; vellum; 23 × 18; 167 leaves; two columns; 22 lines; twelfth century.

7

Συναξάριον ἀπὸ τῶν Εὐαγγελίων· καὶ ἀκολουθιῶν τινων. ἐλλειπὲς τὴν ἀρχὴν καὶ τὸ τέλος· ἐλλειπὲς τὸ δέσιμον· μεμβράνη· κε΄ × κ΄· φύλλα ξθ΄· δίστηλον· γραμμαὶ κε΄· δωδεκάτου αἰῶνος.

Lections from the Gospels and liturgical matter; imperfect at the beginning and end; without binding; vellum; 25 × 20; 69 leaves; two columns; 25 lines; twelfth century.

8

Προφητολόγιον· Εἰς τὸ τέλος εἰσὶ δύο φύλλα συριακῇ τῆς Παλαιστίνης. μεμβράνη· κβ΄ × ιη΄· φύλλα ρλθ΄· μονόστηλον· γραμμαὶ ιδ΄· ὀγδόου αἰῶνος.

Prophetologion; at the end are two pages of Palestinian Syriac; vellum; 22 × 18; 139 leaves; one column; 14 lines; eighth century.

9

Ἑξαήμερον Βασιλείου τοῦ Μεγάλου· ἐλλειπὲς τὸ τέλος·

ܠܐܝ ܐܬܚܪܘܪ

μεμβράνη· κδ΄ × ιϛ΄· φύλλα ριζ΄· δίστηλον· γραμμαὶ κθ΄· στρογγύλη γραφή· ἐννάτου αἰῶνος.

Hexaemeron of Basil the Great; imperfect at the end; vellum; 24 × 16; 117 leaves; two columns; 29 lines; Estrangelo; ninth century.

10

Ὁμιλίαι καὶ ἀποσπάσματα διαφόρων Πατέρων· π.χ.
Ἀμβροσίου τῆς Μεδιολάνου· Ἰακώβου τῆς Σειρούγ· Θεοφί-
λου τῆς Ἀλεξανδρείας· Χρυσοστόμου· Πρόκλου· Ἐφραέμ·
Κυρίλλου τῆς Ἀλεξανδρείας· Ἀναστασίου τῆς Ἀντιοχείας·
Ἰσαὰκ καὶ Τιμοθέου· Ἐπιφανίου καὶ Κορνηλίου. κατὰ τὸ
τέλος σημειώσεις τινὲς περὶ τῶν Ἀποστόλων καὶ Κατάλογοι
ἁγίων βιβλίων· τὰ πάντα τῷ Εἰρηναίῳ ἀποδιδόμενα.

μεμβράνη· ιη΄ × ιγ΄· φύλλα σκδ΄· μονόστηλον· γραμμαὶ
κα΄· ἐννάτου αἰῶνος.

Homilies and Extracts from various Fathers; Ambrose
of Milan, Jacob of Serug, Theophilus of Alexandria, Chrysostom; Proclus, Ephraim, Cyril of Alexandria, Anastasius
of Antioch, Isaac and Timotheus, Epiphanius and Cornelius.
At the end are brief notices of the Apostles and lists of
sacred books ascribed to Irenaeus.

Vellum; 18 × 13; 224 leaves; one column; 21 lines;
ninth century.

Ἀπανθίζομεν τὰ ἀποσπάσματα τὰ ἀκολουθέντα.

The following extracts are from this volume.

SHORT NOTICES OF THE PROPHETS:
from Epiphanius of Cyprus and Cornelius of Jerusalem.

ܓ. ܫܡܘܐܝܠ ܡܢ ܫܒܛܐ ܕܐܦܪܝܡ. ܘܡܫܚܗ
ܘܐܬܡܠܟ ܒܪܡܬܐ. ܒܝܘ̈ܡܝ ܫܐܘܠ

ܕ. ܡ̈ܠܟܐ ܡܫܡܫܢܐ ܀ ܕܘܝܕ ܡܢ ܫܒܛܐ
ܕܝܗܘܕܐ. ܘܚܝܐ ܫܢ̈ܝܢ. ܥ ܘܐܬܡܠܟ

ܗ. ܒܐܘܪܫܠܡ ܀ ܫܬ ܡܢ ܟܬܒ̈ܘܗܝ.
ܘܡܫܚܗ ܘܐܬܡܠܟ ܒܟܬܒ̈ܘܗܝ ܒܝܘ̈ܡܝ

ܘ. ܪܚܒܥܡ ܡ̈ܠܟܐ ܀ ܐܚܝܐ ܬܘܒ

ܙ. ܗܘܐ ܒܝܘ̈ܡܘܗܝ: ܕܪܚܒܥܡ ܀ ܘܐܕ
ܗܘܘ ܡܢ ܫܡܥܘܢ. ܘܠܗ ܡܠܠ
ܐܪܥܐ ܒܝܘ̈ܡܝ ܝܪܒܥܡ ܡܠܟܐ.

ܚ. ܘܐܬܡܠܟ ܒܒܝܬ ܐܝܠ ܀ ܐܠܝܐ
ܗܘܐ ܡܢ ܬܫܒܝ. ܡܢ ܫܒܛܐ ܕܠܘܝ
ܒܝܘ̈ܡܝ ܐܚܒ. ܡܠܟܐ. ܘܒܝܘ̈ܡܝ[1] ܗܢܐ

ܛ. ܠܫܡܝܐ ܐܬܕܒܪ ܀ ܒܡܪܟܒܬܐ ܡܢ ܫܒܛܐ
ܕܐܦܪܝܡ ܘܗܘ ܗܘܐ ܪܒ ܚܝܠܐ
ܕܐܚܒ. ܘܗܘ ܠܘܬ ܡܠܐܟܐ ܢܒܝܐ
ܒܡܕܝܢܬܐ. ܘܗܘܐ ܬܠܡܝܕܗ ܕܐܠܝܐ

ܝ. ܢܒܝܐ: ܝܘܢ ܗܘܐ ܡܢ ܓܬܚܦܪ ܒܪܗ
ܕܡܬܝ. ܘܠܗ ܐܫܕ ܐܠܝܐ ܢܒܝܐ
ܒܗ ܒܪܗ ܒܪܝܬܐ ܕܚܝܘܬܐ ܡ̈ܠܟܐ ܀

ܝܐ. ܐܠܝܫܥ ܗܘܐ ܡܢ ܫܒܛܐ ܕܪܘܒܝܠ
ܘܗܘܐ ܬܠܡܝܕܗ ܕܐܠܝܐ: ܐܫܬܢܝ ܠܐ
ܗܘܐ ܒܝܘ̈ܡܝ ܚܙܩܝܐ ܘܟܬܒ
ܘܐܚܝ ܘܚܙܩܝܐ ܡ̈ܠܟܐ ܕܝܗܘܕܐ

[1] Some words seem to be dropped here.

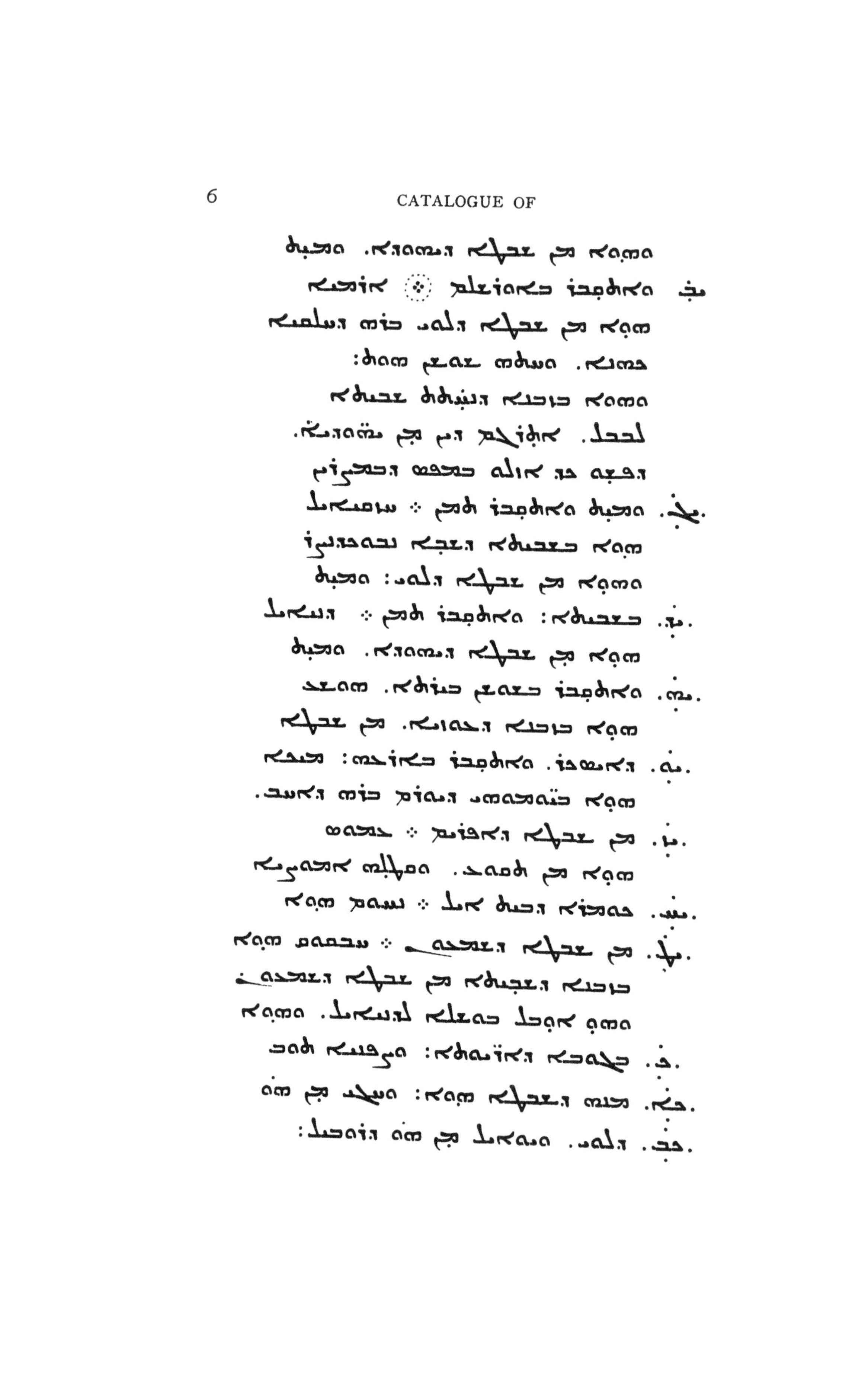

ܡܠܐܟܐ ܕܝܢ ܡܢ ܕܗܠܝܢ ܡܢ ܟܠ
ܐܬܘܬܐ. ܘܗܘܝܢ ܢܒܝܐ. ܐܚܪܢܐ ܀ ܗ̈ܠܝܢ
ܕܝܢ ܒܟܬܒܗ ܐܦܝܦܢܝܘܣ ܕܩܘܦܪܘܣ
ܘܩܘܪܠܘܣ ܕܐܘܪܫܠܡ ܀ ܫܠܡ ܀ ܬܘܒ
ܒ̈. ܡܩܠܐܘܗ̱ ܡܛܠ ܫܠܝܚܐ ܡܪܢܝܐ
ܫܡܥܘܢ ܡܢ ܒܝܬ ܨܝܕܐ ܡܢ ܫܒܛܐ
ܕܢܦܬܠܝ. ܘܡܝܬ ܒܪܗܘܡܐ. ܒܫܢܬ
ܓ̈. ܫܒܛ: ܒܢܝܢ ܣܝܡܢ: ܒܢܫ: ܒܗ: ܐܢܕܪܐܘܣ
ܐܚܘܗܝ ܕܫܡܥܘܢ ܡܝܬ ܒܦܐܛܪܐ
ܕ̈. ܡܕܝܢܬܐ: ܝܥܩܘܒ ܒܪ ܙܒܕܝ ܡܢ ܫܒܛܐ
ܕܙܒܘܠܘܢ. ܡܢ ܩܕܡ ܚܕܐ ܫܢܬܐ
ܕܗܘܠܝܢ ܕܒܪ̈ ܡܫܠܡ ܗܪܘܕܣ:
ܗ̈. ܘܝܘܚܢܢ ܐܚܘܗܝ ܕܝܥܩܘܒ. ܘܡܝܬ
ܒܫܢܬܐ ܕܛܪܝܢܘܣ ܡܠܟܐ ܘܐܬܩܒܪ
ܘ̈. ܒܐܦܣܘܣ: ܦܝܠܝܦܘܣ ܡܢ ܫܒܛܐ ܕܐܫܝܪ
ܡܢ ܒܝܬ ܨܝܕܐ ܘܐܬܩܒܪ ܒܐܝܪܦܘܠܝܣ.
ܙ̈. ܒܪ ܬܘܠܡܝ ܡܢ ܫܒܛܐ ܕܐܝܣܟܪ
ܚ̈. ܘܐܬܩܒܪ ܒܐܠܒܢܘܦܘܠܝܣ: ܬܘܡܐ
ܡܝܬ ܒܩܠܡܝܢܐ ܡܕܝܢܬܐ ܕܗܢܕܘܝܐ
ܛ̈. ܡܬܝ ܡܢ ܫܒܛܐ ܕܐܝܣܟܪ ܡܢ ܢܨܪܬ
ܝ̈. ܡܕܝܢܬܐ. ܘܡܝܬ ܒܗܢܕܘ: ܫܡܥܘܢ ܡܢ
ܫܒܛܐ ܕܐܦܪܝܡ. ܡܢ ܩܛܢܐ ܡܕܝܢܬܐ ܀
ܝ̈ܐ. ܝܗܘܕܐ ܕܐܬܩܪܝ ܬܕܝ. ܕܗܘ ܠܒܝ ܡܢ
ܫܒܛܐ ܕܝܗܘܕܐ. ܘܐܬܩܒܪ ܒܒܝܪܘܬܘܣ ܀
ܝ̈ܒ ܝܥܩܘܒ ܒܪ ܚܠܦܝ. ܡܢ ܫܒܛܐ

Then follows the list of the seventy disciples according to Irenaeus, and a Stichometry of the Old and New Testaments.

Τὰ τῶν ἑβδομήκοντα μαθητῶν ὀνόματα εἰς τὸν Εἰρηναῖον ἀποδιδόμενα.
Στιχομετρία τῆς παλαιᾶς διαθήκης καὶ τῆς καινῆς.

This catalogue of the Seventy Disciples must be compared with similar lists in Greek MSS., where they are commonly referred to Hippolytus. As before, we set up the text, line for line, from the MS.

Irenaeus, p. 1.   ....

ܘܐܬܬܣܝܡ ܬܡܢ : ܘ : ܣܘܣܬܢܝܣ
ܗܝܢ ܕܟܬܒ ܦܘܠܘܣ : ܙ : ܦܪܘܣܘܦܘܣ
ܡܬܒܬ ܡܢ ܕܒܪܐ ܒܐܠܟܣܢܕܪܝܐ: ܚ : ܩܘܦܐ
ܒܠܘܩܐ ܕܐܬܘܗܝ ܠܦܘܠܝܐ ܕܒܝܠܬܗ
ܡܚܒ ܡܢܝ̈ ܦܓܪܗ ܘܟܢܫ ܕܒܗ. ܠܐ :
ܢܩܘܕܝܡܘܣ ܦܪܝܫܐ : ܛ : ܢܬܢܐܝܠ ܪܝܫܐ
ܕܣܦܪ̈ܐ: ܡܬܝܐ ܗܘ ܕܗܘ̣ܐ ܚܠܦ
ܝܗܘܕܐ: ܝܐ: ܝܘܣܛܘܣ: ܝܒ: ܝܗܘܕܐ
ܐܚܘܗܝ ܕܡܪܢ: ܝܓ: ܫܠܝܐ: ܝܕ:
ܝܗܘܕܐ ܒܪ ܫܒܐ: ܝܗ: ܡܪܘܣܘܣ: ܝܘ:
ܘܫܠܡ: ܝܙ: ܡܫܘܚ ܘܦܣܩܐ: ܝܚ:
ܬܫܒܘܚܬܐ: ܝܛ: ܡܪܘܕܘܣ: ܟ: ܢܝܓܪ: ܟܐ:
ܐܘܚܕ: ܟܒ: ܪܘܦܘܣ: ܟܓ: ܐܠܟܣܢܕܪܘܣ:
ܟܕ: ܫܘܒܚܐ ܘܩܘܪܒܢܐ ܕܗ̣ܘܐ

Irenaeus, p. 2. ܐܒܘܗܝ: ܟܗ: ܠܦܘܠܘܣ ܕܡܢ ܩܘܪܒܢܐ:
ܟܘ: ܫܠܘܡܐ ܐܚܘܗܝ ܕܦܘܠܘܣ: ܟܙ:
ܫܘܒܚܐ ܒܪܗ ܕܗ̣ܘܐ ܐܦܝܣܩܘܦܐ
ܒܐܘܪܫܠܡ. ܘܐܬܩܛܠ ܒܪ ܩܝ: ܫܢܝܢ.
ܒܐܘܪܫܠܡ: ܟܚ: ܢܣܡܒ ܐܚܘܗܝ ܕܡܪܢ:
ܟܛ: ܝܗܘܕܐ ܕܐܬܩܪܝ ܫܘܒܚܐ: ܠ:
ܐܘܪܚܐ ܀ ܘܗ̈ܠܝܢ ܕܐ̇ܘܠܝܢ ܗ̈ܘܘ ܟܡ
ܠܘܩܒܠ ܒܐܘܪܚܐ. ܕܐܬܚܫܒܘ ܗ̈ܠܝܢ.
ܠܐ: ܬܘܪܣܝܣ: ܠܒ: ܘܩܘܦܪ: ܠܓ..
ܒܪ̈ܝܗ ܀ ܘܗ̈ܠܝܢ ܫܒܥܐ ܡܫ̈ܡܫܢܐ
ܠܕ: ܐܣܛܦܢܘܣ ܕܐܬܪܓܡ: ܠܗ:

ܦܝܠܝܦܘܣ ܕܐܬܠܡܕ ܠܫܡܥܘܢ. ܠܗ.
ܦܪܘܟܪܘܣ: ܠܘ: ܢܝܩܢܘܪ: ܠܙ: ܦܪܡܢܐ
ܠܛ: ܛܝܡܘܢ: ܡ: ܢܝܩܠܐܘܣ ܓܝܘܪܐ
ܘܗܠܝܢ ܕܡܬܒܕܪܝܢ ܒܦܠܓܘܗ ܕܗܘܘ
ܒܪܢܒܐ: ܡܐ: ܐܢܕܪܘܢܝܩܘܣ. ܡܒ.
ܡܢܣܐ: ܡܓ: ܛܛܘܣ. ܡܕ: ܦܛܪܒܐ:
ܡܗ: ܗܪܡܐ: ܡܘ: ܦܠܓܘܢ: ܡܙ:
ܐܣܘܢܩܪܝܛܘܣ: ܡܚ: ܗܪܡܐ: ܚܢܢܐ
ܕܡܫܡܫܝܢ ܠܗ ܪܒܢܐ: ܘܬܠܬܐ ܬܘܒ
ܐܚܪ̈ܢܐ. ܗܘܘ ܥܡ ܦܛܪܘܣ ܒܡܫܪܝܐ
ܡܛ: ܟܪܝܣܩܣ: ܢ: ܩܠܝܡܝܣ: ܢܐ: ܩܪܦܘ:
ܢܒ: ܥܒܘܠܐ: ܢܓ: ܓܐܝܘܣ

Irenaeus, p. 3. ܐܒܠܘܣ: ܘܗܠܝܢ ܬܘܒ ܕܟܦܪܘ
ܗܘ ܒܡܫܝܚܐ ܡܢܗܘܢ ܡܬܚܫܒܝܢ
ܕܐܬܚܫܒܘܢ: ܢܗ: ܩܪܝܬܘܣ ܀ ܢܘ:
ܐܒܝܘܢ: ܟܠܘ ܕܝܢ ܫܠܝܚܘܗܝ: ܢܙ:
ܠܘܩܐ ܐܘܢܓܠܣܛܐ: ܢܚ: ܐܦܠܐ
ܟܝܢܐ: ܢܛ: ܐܘܪܒܢܘܣ: ܣ: ܐܣܛܟܘܣ.
ܗܐ: ܦܘܦܠܝܘܣ: ܣܒ: ܐܪܝܣܛܘܒܘܠܘܣ
ܣܓ: ܐܣܦܝܢܐ: ܣܕ: ܗܪܘܕܝܘܢ: ܣܗ:
ܢܪܩܝܣܘܣ: ܣܘ: ܪܘܦܘܣ: ܣܙ: ܐܠܡܦܐ.
ܣܚ: ܘܢܪܩܝܣܘܣ: ܣܛ: ܐܚܕ: ܥ:
ܫܡܗܝܗܘܢ: ܥܠ ܫܡܗܐ ܕܐܘܢܓܠܣܛܐ: Names of the Evangelists
ܐ. ܡܬܝ ܡܢ ܝܗܘܕ: ܘܡܠܠ ܥܒܪܐܝܬ
ܒ. ܒܠܛܝܢܐ: ܡܪܩܘܣ ܡܢ ܫܡܥܘܢ

Catalogue of
Canonical
Books

Genesis =
4516 verses

Exodus =
3378 verses

Irenaeus, p. 4.

Leviticus
= 2684 verses

Numbers
= 3481 verses

Deuteronomy
= 2982 verses

Total for
Pentateuch
17041 verses

Joshua
= 1953 verses

Judges
= 2088 verses

Samuel
= 3436 verses

Kings
= 6113 verses

2—2

ܘܬܠܬܡܐܐ: ܪܥܘܬ: ܡܐ̈ܬܝܢ — Ruth = 246 verses

ܘܐܪ̈ܒܥܝܢ ܘܫܬܐ ܦܬܓ̈ܡܐ ܕܕܘܝܕ. — David = 4830

ܦܬܓܡܐ ܐܪ̈ܒܥܐ ܐ̈ܠܦܝܢ ܘܬ̈ܡܢܡܐܐ

ܘܬܠܬܝܢ ܗܦܟ ܕܒܪܝܡܝܢ ܦܬܓ̈ܡܐ — Chronicles = 3553

ܬܠܬܐ ܐ̈ܠܦܝܢ ܘܚܡܫܡܐܐ ܘܚܡ̈ܫܝܢ

ܘܬܠܬܐ: ܐܝܘܒ: ܦܬܓ̈ܡܐ ܐܠܦ. — Job = 1548

ܘܚܡ̈ܫܡܐܐ ܘܐܪ̈ܒܥܝܢ ܘܬܡܢܝܐ

Irenaeus, p. 5. ܫܒܥܡܐܐ ܕܡ̈ܬܠܐ ܦ̈ܬܓܡܐ — Prov. = 1762

ܐܠܦ ܘܫ̈ܒܥܡܐܐ ܫ̈ܬܝܢ ܘܬ̈ܪܝܢ

ܬܪ̈ܥܣܪ ܦ̈ܬܓܡܐ ܬܠܬܐ ܐ̈ܠܦܝܢ — Twelve (minor Prophets) = 3643

ܘܫ̈ܬܡܐܐ ܘܐܪ̈ܒܥܝܢ ܘܬܠܬܐ

ܐܫܥܝܐ ܦ̈ܬܓܡܐ ܬܠܬܐ ܐܠܦܝܢ — Isaiah = 3656

ܘܫܬܡܐܐ ܘܚܡܫܝܢ ܘܫܬܐ ܐܪܡܝܐ: — Jeremiah = 4252

ܦ̈ܬܓܡܐ ܐܪ̈ܒܥܐ ܐܠܦܝܢ ܘܡܐܬܝܢ

ܘܚܡܫܝܢ ܘܬ̈ܪܝܢ ܐܘܠܝܬܗ ܦܬܓ̈ܡܐ — Lamentations = 433

ܐܪܒܥܡܐܐ ܘܬܠܬܝܢ ܘܬܠܬܐ

ܦܬܓܡܝܢ: ܕܕܢܝܐܝܠ ܦܬܓ̈ܡܐ ܐܠܦ — Daniel = 1555

ܚܡܫܡܐܐ ܘܚܡܫܝܢ ܘܚܡܫܐ

ܚܙܩܝܐܝܠ ܦܬܓ̈ܡܐ ܐܪܒܥܐ ܐܠܦܝܢ — Ezekiel = 4376

ܘܬܠܬܡܐܐ ܘܫܒ̈ܥܝܢ ܘܫܬܐ:

ܐܣܬܝܪ: ܦܬܓ̈ܡܐ ܫܬܡܐܐ — Esther = 650

ܘܚܡܫܝܢ: ܥܙܪܐ ܦ̈ܬܓܡܐ ܬܪ̈ܝܢ — Ezra 2308

ܐܠܦܝܢ ܘܬܠܬܡܐܐ ܘܬܡܢܝܐ

ܡܩܒܝܐ ܩܕܡܝܐ ܕܡܩܒ̈ܝܐ: — 1 Macc. = 2766

ܦ̈ܬܓܡܐ ܬܪ̈ܝܢ ܐ̈ܠܦܝܢ ܘܫܒܥܡܐܐ

ܘܫ̈ܬܝܢ ܘܫܬܐ: ܡܩܒܝܐ ܕܬܪ̈ܝܢ

ܕܡܩܒܝܐ: ܦܬ̈ܓܡܐ ܚܡܫܐ ܐܠܦܝܢ 2 Macc. = 5600

ܘܫ̈ܬܡܐܐ: ܕܝܗܘܕܝܬ ܦܬ̈ܓܡܐ Judith = 1268

Irenaeus, p. 6. ܐܠܦ ܘܡܐܬܝܢ ܘܫ̈ܬܝܢ ܘܬܡܢܝܐ:

ܚܟܡܬܐ ܪܒܬܐ ܦܬ̈ܓܡܐ ܐܠܦ Sap. Sol. = 1550

ܘܚܡܫܡܐܐ ܘܚܡܫܝܢ: ܒܪ ܐܣܝܪܐ: Sap. Sir. = 2550

ܦܬ̈ܓܡܐ ܬܪ̈ܝܢ ܐ̈ܠܦܝܢ ܘܚܡܫܡܐܐ:

ܘܚܡܫܝܢ: ܟܠܗ̇ ܕܥܬܝܩܬܐ ܟܬܒܘܬܐ Total for Old Testament = 71,574

ܐ̈ܠܦܐ ܫ̈ܒܥܝܢ ܘܚܕ ܘܚܡܫܡܐܐ

ܘܫܒܥܝܢ ܘܐܪ̈ܒܥܐ ܦܬ̈ܓܡܝܢ: ܐܘܢܓܠܝܘܢ Matthew = 2522

ܕܡܬܝ ܦܬ̈ܓܡܐ ܬܪ̈ܝܢ ܐ̈ܠܦܝܢ

ܘܚܡܫܡܐܐ ܘܥܣܪܝܢ ܘܬܪ̈ܝܢ ܀

ܐܘܢܓܠܝܘܢ ܕܡܪܩܘܣ: ܦܬ̈ܓܡܐ Mark = 1675

ܐܠܦ ܘܫ̈ܬܡܐܐ ܘܫ̈ܒܥܝܢ ܘܚܡܫܐ:

ܐܘܢܓܠܝܘܢ ܕܠܘܩܐ: ܦܬ̈ܓܡܐ ܬܠܬܐ Luke = 3083

ܐܠܦܝܢ ܘܬܡܢܝܢ ܘܬܠܬܐ: ܐܘܢܓܠܝܘܢ John = 1737

ܕܝܘܚܢܢ ܦܬ̈ܓܡܐ ܐܠܦ ܘܫܒܥܡܐܐ

ܘܬ̈ܠܬܝܢ ܘܫܒܥܐ: ܟܠܗ ܐܘܢܓܠܝܘܢ: Total four Gospels = 9218

ܦܬ̈ܓܡܐ ܬܫܥܐ ܐܠܦܝܢ ܘܡܐܬ̈ܝܢ

ܘܬܡܢܬܥܣܪ: ܦܪܟܣܝܣ ܕܫܠܝ̈ܚܐ Acts = 2720

ܦܬ̈ܓܡܐ ܬܪ̈ܝܢ ܐܠܦܝܢ ܘܫܒܥܡܐܐ:

ܘܥܣܪ̈ܝܢ ܕܦܘܠܘܣ ܫܠܝܚܐ ܐܓܪ̈ܬܐ

ܕܓܠܛܝܐ ܦܬ̈ܓܡܐ ܡܐܬ̈ܝܢ ܘܫ̈ܬܝܢ Galatians = 265

ܘܚܡܫܐ: ܕܩܘܪܢܬܝܐ ܩܕܡܝܬܐ 1 Corinthians = 946

Irenaeus, p. 7. ܦܬ̈ܓܡܐ ܬܫܥܡܐܐ ܘܐܪ̈ܒܥܝܢ ܘܫܬܐ:

ܕܩܘܪܢܬܝܐ ܕܬܪ̈ܬܝܢ: ܦܬ̈ܓܡܐ 2 Corinthians = 653

ܬ̈ܡܢܡܐܐ ܫܒܥܝܢ ܘܬܠܬܐ

ܕܪ̈ܗܘܡܝܐ ܦ̈ܬܓܡܐ ܬ̈ܡܢܡܐܐ ܘܥܣܪ̈ܝܢ Romans = 825

ܘܚܡ̈ܫܐ ܕܥܒܪ̈ܝܐ: ܦ̈ܬܓܡܐ ܬ̈ܡܢܡܐܐ Hebrews = 837

ܘܬܠܬܝܢ ܘܫܒܥܐ: ܕܩܘܠܣܝܐ Colossians = 275

ܦ̈ܬܓܡܐ ܡܐܬ̈ܝܢ ܘܫ̈ܒܥܝܢ ܘܚܡ̈ܫܐ

ܕܐܦܣܝܐ ܦ̈ܬܓܡܐ ܬܠ̈ܬܡܐܐ Ephesians = 318?

ܘܬܡܢܬܥܣܪ: ܕܦܝܠܝܦܣܝܐ ܦ̈ܬܓܡܐ Philippians = 318

ܬܠܬܡܐܐ ܘ̈ܬܡܢܬܥܣܪ: ܕܦܝܠܝܦܣܝܐ: Philippians (iterum) = 235

ܦ̈ܬܓܡܐ ܡܐܬ̈ܝܢ ܘ̈ܬܠܬܝܢ ܘܚܡܫܐ:

ܕܬܣܠܘ̈ܢܝܩܝܐ: ܡܕܝܢܬܐ ܦ̈ܬܓܡܐ 1 Thess. = 417 (!)

ܐܪ̈ܒܥܡܐܐ ܘܫܒܥܬܥܣܪ: ܕܬܣܠܘ̈ܢܝܩܝܐ 2 Thess. = 118

ܕܬܪ̈ܬܝܢ: ܦ̈ܬܓܡܐ ܡܐܐ ܘܬܡܢܬܥܣܪ:

ܠܛܝܡܬܐܘܣ: ܕܬܪ̈ܬܝܢ: ܦ̈ܬܓܡܐ 2 Tim. = 114

ܡܐܐ ܘܐܪܒܥܬܥܣܪ: ܕܛܛܘܣ: ܦ̈ܬܓܡܐ Titus = 116

ܡܐܐ ܘܫ̈ܬܬܥܣܪ: ܕܦܝܠܝܡܘܢ: ܚܡ̈ܫܝܢ Philemon = 53

ܘܬܠܬܐ: ܟܠܗ ܫܠܝܚܐ: ܦ̈ܬܓܡܐ Total for Apostle = 5076

ܚܡ̈ܫܐ ܐ̈ܠܦܝܢ ܘܫ̈ܒܥܝܢ ܘܫܬܐ: ܟܠܗܘܢ

ܟܬ̈ܒܐ: ܩ̈ܒܝܥܐ ܕܡܫܠܡܐ ܒܥܕܬܐ Total for books received by the Church = 90,000

ܡܕܝܢܬܐ: ܬܫ̈ܥܝܢ ܐ̈ܠܦܝܢ: ܦ̈ܬܓܡܐ:

Irenaeus, p. 8. ܘܬܘܒ ܕܗܠܝܢ ܐܝܟ ܢ̈ܒܝܐ ܕܠܐ

ܐܬܟܬܒܘ ܦܦ̈ܝܪܘܢ ܠܒܪ ܡܢ ܗ̈ܢܘܢ

ܕܐܬܟܬܒܘ: ܣܒܪܝܢ ܗ̈ܠܝܢ ܕܐܬܢܒܝܘ

ܒܢܡܘܣܐ. ܘܒܟܬܒܐ ܕܢ̈ܒܝܐ ܕܦܠܓ

ܬܠܬ ܒܡܐܘܠ ܡ̈ܠܟܐ: ܘܡ̈ܐܬܐ ܢ̈ܒܝܐ

ܕܦܫܝ ܗܘܐ ܒܡܕܝܢܬܐ: ܙܒ ܒܢܬܐ

ܡܟܝܪܬܐ. ܘܗܢܘ ܒܪ ܣܒܪܐ. ܗܢܐ ܗܘ
ܘܢܦܩ ܗܘܐ ܩܕܡ ܠܒܘܠܐ ܐܘܟ ܒܝܠܐ
ܩܝܡ ܠܚܝܐ ܗܘ ܐܝܟܪܝ ܐܝܟܪܬ ܠܐܘܐ:

etc.   etc.

The foregoing document deserves the elucidation of a few notes.

p. 1, init. Although ascribed to Irenaeus, the list is suspiciously Edessan, at all events in its arrangement; for the first name amongst the Seventy is *Adar* who died in *Urhai*; this must be the Edessan Apostle *Addai*.

p. 1, l. 12. The tradition that the last supper took place in Joseph's upper room should be remarked.

p. 1, l. 14. Nathanael is described as the chief of the scribes; it is curious that he is similarly described in the Diatessaron of Tatian ('a scribe, a true Israelite').

p. 2, l. 7. The names of the *three* (sic!) who accompanied Cleophas to Emmaus must rest on some apocryphal tradition (Thyrsis, Castor and Zabrion (?)): in the Curetonian Syriac and the Old Latin texts the names are two only, viz. Cleophas and Emmaus.

p. 2, l. 14. The writer betrays his source in Rom. xvi. for the names which follow, and apparently (for the spelling of the names agrees fairly with that of the Peshito) it is a Syriac text of Romans that he uses. The reason, in the first instance, for taking names of the Seventy from the Salutations in Romans, is that Andronicus and Junia[s] are called *apostles* who were in Christ before Paul.

p. 2, l. 19. The second ܩܘܪܐ is called ܪܥܝܐ; this is evidently a corruption of ܪܥܝܐ (shepherd).

p. 2, l. 20. Six names are given of apostolic men who were with Peter in Caesarea; cf. Acts xvi. 12 "These six brethren accompanied me": but the source of their names is obscure.

p. 3, l. 5. The substitutes for Cerinthus and Ebion are Luke the Evangelist and ܐܠܐ the Chosen: apparently this is meant for Luke and Apollos; but it is the spelling of the Peshito for *Apelles* the Chosen in Rom. xvi. 10. The writer has misunderstood the Syriac name; but that he is working on Romans is clear not only from the coincidence in the name and title, but from the fact that he immediately incorporates more names from the same list.

The whole document is suspiciously Syrian in origin. The ascription to Irenaeus may perhaps be due to the insertion of the document on blank leaves at the end of some copy of the works of Irenaeus. J. R. H.

11

Τὰ τέσσαρα Εὐαγγέλια· κατὰ τὴν μετάφρασιν Πεσσίτο. μεμβράνη· κβ′ × ιδ′· φύλλα ριη′· δίστηλον· γραμμαὶ λ′· ἐννάτου αἰῶνος.

The four Gospels, according to the Peshito version; vellum; 22 × 14; 118 leaves; two columns; 30 lines; ninth century.

12

Τὸ Εὐαγγέλιον κατὰ Λουκᾶν· κατὰ τὴν μετάφρασιν Πεσσίτο. ἐλλειπὲς τὴν ἀρχὴν καὶ τὸ τέλος· κατηρτισμένον ἐπὶ χάρτου ὑπὸ νεωτέρας χειρὸς εἰς τὴν ἀρχήν. Τὸ κείμενον ἔχει βραχεῖς προλόγους καθ᾽ ἕκαστον ἀνάγνωσμα.

μεμβράνη· κγ′ × ιδ′· φύλλα ρλε′· ὧν μζ′ χάρτινα· μονόστηλον· γραμμαὶ κγ′· στρογγύλη γραφή· ἑβδόμου αἰῶνος.

The Gospel of Luke according to the Peshito; imper-

fect at the beginning and end. A later hand has restored
it on paper at the beginning. The text has short prefaces
for the successive lections.

88 leaves of vellum, and 47 of paper; 23 × 14; one
column; 23 lines; Estrangelo; seventh century.

13

Ἀναγνώσματα ἀπὸ τῶν Εὐαγγελίων καὶ τῶν Ἐπιστολῶν.
μεμβράνη· κ΄ × ιγ΄· φύλλα σλβ΄· γραμμαὶ κα΄· ἐνδεκάτου
αἰῶνος.

Lections from the Gospels and Epistles; vellum;
20 × 13; 232 leaves; 21 lines; eleventh century.

14

ܪܫܝܕܐܠܝܢ ܐܝܟ ܪܫܝܕܐ ܪܕܐ ܡܢ ܪܫܝܢܣ
ܩܝܢܡܝ ܪܝܢ ܪܫܝܢ ܡܢ ܕܐܪܫܝܢ ܪܕܐܝܢ

Μακάριος, ('Ιωάννης ܩܢ ܠܝܢ) Ἰσαὰκ, Γρεγ. Ναζιανζ.,
ἀκολουθέντες διὰ λόγων τινῶν τῶν Φιλοσόφων· π.χ. Θεμι-
στίου· Πλάτωνος· Ἀριστοτέλους· βίου τοῦ Ἁγίου Διονυσίου·
Σεραπείου· Ἰουλίου τῆς Ῥώμης· Ἰουστίνου.

μεμβράνη· κα΄ × ιε΄· φύλλα ρπα΄· μονόστηλον· γραμμαὶ
κε΄· δεκάτου αἰῶνος.

Extracts from Macarius, (John of ܩܢ ܠܝܢ) Isaac,
Greg. Nazianz., followed by sayings of the Philosophers,
Themistius, Plato, Aristotle, Life of St Dionysius, Sera-
pion, Julius of Rome, Justin.

Vellum; 21 × 15; 181 leaves; one column; 25 lines;
tenth century.

15

Περιέχει τὰς Πράξεις τῶν Ἀποστόλων, τὰς Καθολικὰς
Ἐπιστολὰς, καὶ τὰς τοῦ Ἁγίου Παύλου (αἱ τελευταῖαί εἰσι

δίστηλοι). Φύλλα τινὰ ἐπὶ παλιμψήστου κατηρτισμένα, τοῦ ὑποκειμένου συριακοῦ ὄντος. Τὰ δὲ φύλλα τοῦ παλιμψήστου ἐστὶν ἐν μέρει ἀπὸ τοῦ Λευιτικοῦ, καὶ ἐν μέρει ἀπὸ βιβλίου προσευχῶν ἢ ὕμνων τῇ Παναγίᾳ. Ἐπὶ τοῦ δεσίμου κεῖται ἓν φύλλον ἐν συριακῇ τῆς Παλαιστίνης γεγραμμένον, περιέχει τεμάχιον τοῦ βιβλίου Ἰώβ (μοναδικόν ἐστι).

μεμβράνη· κγ΄ × ιϛ΄· φύλλα σλε΄· μονόστηλον· γραμμαὶ κγ΄· ὀγδόου αἰῶνος.

Contains the Acts of the Apostles, the Catholic and Pauline Epistles (the latter in two columns). Some leaves restored on palimpsest with the Syriac writing beneath. The palimpsest leaves are partly from the Old Testament, and partly from a book of prayers and hymns to the Virgin. In the cover is a leaf of Palestinian Syriac containing a fragment of the book of Job.

Vellum; 23 × 16; 235 leaves; one column; 23 lines; eighth century.

16

Περιέχει (α΄) τοὺς βίους τῶν Αἰγυπτιακῶν Πατέρων. (β΄) τὸν βίον τοῦ Ἁγίου Νείλου τοῦ Ἀναχωρίτου. (γ΄) τὴν Ἀπολογίαν τοῦ Ἀριστείδου ὑπὲρ τῶν χριστιανῶν (φύλλ.... Ϟγ΄...ρε΄). (δ΄) λόγον τοῦ Πλουτάρχου περὶ τοῦ εὐεργετηθῆναι ὑπὸ τῶν ἐχθρῶν. (ε΄) τοῦ αὐτοῦ Πλουτάρχου περὶ ἀσκήσεως. (ϛ΄) λόγον τοῦ Πυθαγόρου. (ζ΄) τοῦ Πλουτάρχου περὶ ὀργῆς. (η΄) τοῦ Λουκιανοῦ περὶ τοῦ μὴ ῥαδίως πιστεύειν διαβολῇ. (θ΄) λόγον Φιλοσόφου τινὸς περὶ ψυχῆς. (ι΄) τὴν συμβουλὴν Θεάνω τῆς μαθητρίας τοῦ Πυθαγόρου. (ια΄) λόγους τῶν Φιλοσόφων. (ιβ΄) σχόλιον εἰς Ἐκκλησιαστὴν ὑπὸ τοῦ Ἁγίου Ἰωάννου τοῦ Ἀναχωρίτου. (ιγ΄) σχόλια τοῦ Ἰωάννου Χρυσοστόμου εἰς Ματθαῖον.

μεμβράνη· μονόστηλον μέχρι φύλλου Ϟγ΄· ἔπειτα δίστηλον· γραμμαὶ λα΄· στρογγύλη γραφή· τοῦ ἑβδόμου αἰῶνος.

Contains (1) the lives of the Egyptian Fathers, fol. 1—
86. (2) The Life of the Holy Nilus the Anchorite, fol. 87—
93. (3) The Apology of Aristides on behalf of the Christians, fol. 93—105. (4) A discourse of Plutarch on the
advantage to be derived from one's enemies, fol. 105—112.
(5) A discourse of the same Plutarch about asceticism,
fol. 112—121. (6) A discourse of Pythagoras, fol. 121—
126. (7) A discourse of Plutarch about anger, fol. 126—
132. (8) A discourse of Lucian that we should not
readily believe slander against our friends, fol. 132—140.
(9) Discourse of a Philosopher about the Soul, fol. 140—143.

[Syriac text in two columns, with marginal notes "fol. 140 a" and "fol. 140 b"]

---

a Sic in codice, rescribe [Syriac] vel [Syriac]

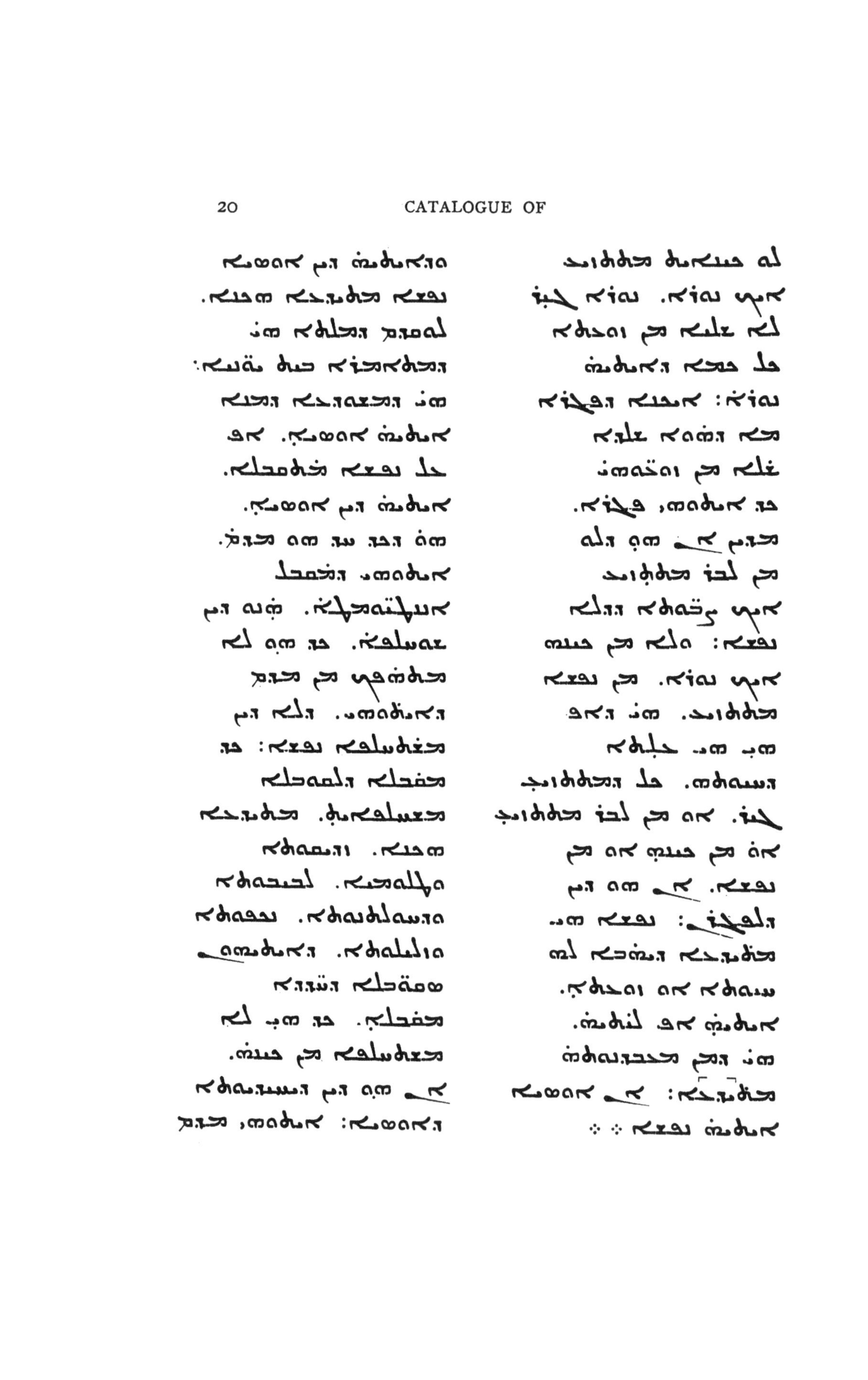

 fol.
141 a

ܡܢ ܡܥܡܕܢܘܬܗ
ܕܦܓܪܗ̇. ܚܢܢܐ ܗܘ̣.
ܦܓܪ. ܗܘܕܥܐ ܓܝܪ
ܡܫܘܚܐ ܗܘ.
ܡ̈ܫܘܚܐ ܕܝܢ ܡܫܬܪܝܢܐ
ܗܘ. ܡܫܬܪܝܢܐ ܕܝܢ
ܡܪܒܒܢܐ ܗܘ. ܡܪܒܒܢܐ
ܕܝܢ ܬܠܬܐ ܩܢܘ̈ܡܝܢ ܐܝܬ
ܠܗ. ܡܕܡ ܕܝܢ ܕܐܝܬ
ܠܗ ܬܠܬܐ ܩܢܘ̈ܡܝܢ
ܦܓܪܐ ܗܘ. ܦܓܪܐ ܕܝܢ
ܟܠ ܦܓܪܐ ܐܟ̄
ܬܬܘܣܦ ܘܣܘܪܐ
ܚܒܪ. ܢܦܫܐ ܕܝܢ ܗ̇ܝ
ܕܐܝܬܝܗ̇ ܒܦܓܪܗ̇.
ܘܣܘܪܗ̇ ܠܐ ܚܒܪܐ.
ܐܠܐ ܡܚܝܢܘ ܡܚܝܢܐ fol. 141 b
ܠܗ̇. ܡܕܡ ܠܗ ܦܓܪܐ
ܐܝܬܝܗ̇. ܐܠܐ ܕܕܠܐ
ܓܫܡ ܗܘ̇. ܐܟ̄
ܓܘܫܡܐ ܗܘ ܓܝܪ
ܢܦܫܐ: ܐܘ ܡܢ ܠܒܪ
ܡܬܬܙܝܥܢܐ ܐܘ ܡܢ ܠܓܘ.
ܠܐ ܕܝܢ ܡܢ ܠܒܪ
ܡܬܬܙܝܥܢܐ. ܠܐ ܓܝܪ
ܡܬܚܙܝܢܐ ܘܠܐ ܡܬܚܙܝܢܐ.

ܐܝܟ ܪ̈ܓܘܬܐ ܕܕܠܐ
ܢܦܫܐ. ܘܠܐ ܬܘܒ ܡܢ
ܠܒܪ ܡܬܬܙܝܥܢܐ ܐܝܟ
ܦܓܪܐ ܢܦܫܢܐ: ܕܢܦܫܐ
ܗܘ ܡܙܝܥܢܐ ܠܗ. ܠܐ
ܓܝܪ ܗ̇ܠܐ ܕܢܦܫܐ ܕܢܦܫܐ
ܢܡܟܪ. ܡܕܡ ܠܗ ܦܓܪܐ
ܗܝ ܐܠܐ ܕܕܠܐ ܦܓܪ.
ܐܟ̄ ܓܘܫܡܐ ܗܘ̇
ܢܦܫܐ̇. ܐܦ ܒܕ̈ܝܢܗ̇
ܦܓܪ̈ܢܐ ܐܝܟ ܐܦ
ܡܬܬܪܣܝܐ. ܘܐܟ̄
ܡܣܬܒܪܐ̇. ܠܗ̇
ܦܓܪܢܝܬ ܡܣܬܒܪܐ
ܐܝܟ ܦܓܪܐ̇. ܐܠܐ̇
ܕܕܠܐ ܓܫܡ. ܒܡܠܬܐ
ܗܘ ܓܝܪ ܡܣܬܒܪܐ.
ܘܠܐ ܒܥ̈ܝܢܝܢ ܡܬܚܙܝܢܐ.
ܠܐ ܓܝܪ ܕܪܘܚܢܝܬܐ
ܡܬܡܫܚܐ̇. ܘܠܐ ܠܡܫܘܚܬܐ̇.
ܘܠܐ ܡܕܡ ܕܐܝܟ
ܗܠܝܢ. ܗܠܝܢ ܕܐܝܬܝܗܘܢ̄
ܓ̈ܫܫܐ ܕܢܦܫܐ. ܡܕܡ
[ܠܗ] ܦܓܪܐ ܗܘ̣ ܐܠܐ
ܕܕܠܐ ܓܫܡ ܕܐܟ̄
ܦܣܩܬܐ ܐܝܬܝܗ̇ ܢܦܫܐ

ܡܬܚܘܝܢܐ ܕܦܫܝܛܘܬܐ
ܗܘ ܢܦܫܟ. ܡܢ ܗܘ.
ܕܕܠܐ ܓܘܫܡ ܐܝܬܝܟ.
ܐܝܟ ܓܒܪ ܠܘ ܦܓܪܐ ܗܘ:
ܦܓܪܐ ܕܝܢ ܡܪܟܒܐ ܗܘ:
ܡܕܡ ܕܝܢ ܕܡܪܟܒ ܡܢ
ܡܢܘ̈ܬܐ ܡܬܦܠܓ: ܗܘܝ
ܕܝܢ ܕܠܐ ܓܘܫܡ ܐܝܬܝܗ̇:
ܟܕܝܢ ܐܦܠܐ ܡܪܟܒܘܬܐ
ܗܝ. ܦܫܝܛܘܬܐ ܗܝ.
ܗܟܝܠ. ܐܝܟ ܠܐ ܡܢܝܢܬܐ
ܢܦܫܐ: ⁘ ܢܡܦܐܬ
ܐܝܬܝܗ̇ ܦܫܝܛܬܐ. ܗ̇ܝ
ܕܝܢ ܠܐ ܡܪܟܒܘܬ
ܘܠܐ ܡܢܘܬܘܬܐ.
ܘܐܝܠܝܢ. ܫܡܥ.
ܠܝܬ ܡܕܡ ܕܗܘ ܠܢܦܫܗ
ܡܫܚܠ. ܘܐܝܟ ܕܝܢ ܠܟ
ܐܦ ܠܐ ܡܢ ܒܪܫܝܬ
ܡܬܦܢܐ ܗܘܐ. ܡܕܡ
ܒܪ ܕܡܬܚܒܠ ܡܢ
ܗܘܠܐ ܗܘ ܡܬܚܒܠ.
ܡܛܠ ܗܢܐ ܟܠ
ܕܡܬܚܒܠ ܡܫܬܪܝܢܐ
ܗܘ. ܘܡܫܬܪܝܢ
ܡܪܟܒܐ ܗܘ. ܡܪܟܒܐ

ܕܝܢ ܦܠܓ ܡܢܘ̈ܬܐ ܗܘ.
ܘܡܕܡ ܕܐܬܓܫܡ ܡܢ
ܦܠܓܘܬ ܡܢܘ̈ܬܐ.
ܡܢ ܗ̈ܕܡܐ ܡ̈ܫܠܦܐ
ܐܬܓܫܡ. ܫܘܚܠܦܐ
(fol. 142 a) ܕܝܢ ܠܐ ܩܒܠ ܠܢܦܫܗ.
ܠܘ ܒܪ ܚܕ ܗܘ ܡܕܡ.
ܟܕܝܢ ܢܦܫܐ ܕܦܫܝܛܐܝܬ
ܐܝܬܝܗ̇: ܘܠܘ ܡܢ
ܡܢܘ̈ܬܐ ܦܠܓܘܬܐ
ܐܝܬܝܗ̇. ܠܐ ܡܪܟܒܘܬܐ
ܘܠܐ ܡܫܬܪܝܢܘܬܐ
ܐܝܬܝܗ̇. ܘܡܛܠ ܗܢܐ
ܠܐ ܡܝܘܬܐ ܘܠܐ ܡܬܚܒܠܐ
ܬܘܒ ܕܝܢ ܟܠ ܝܘܡ ܕܡܢ
ܡܕܡ ܡܬܬܕܒܪܢܐ ܘܠܐ
ܡܢ ܡܬܗ: ܠܝܬ ܠܗ̇ ܕܝܢ
ܫܘܬܦܘܬ̇ ܐܝܠܐ ܐܝܟ ܡܢ
ܗܘ̇ ܕܡܬܒܥܐ ܠܗ̇. ܗܟܢܐ
ܗܟܢܐ ܡܬܦܫܩܐ ܐܝܟ
ܒܡܐ ܕܡܬܠܒܫܐ ܡܢ
ܚܠܐ ܕܡܒܕܕܢܘܬܗ
ܕܗܘ̇ ܕܩܫܝܐ ܠܗ̇. ܡܟܐ
ܕܝܢ ܕܫܠܝ ܠܗ ܗܘ̇ ܕܩܒܒܕ
ܠܗ̇ ܫܚܝ. ܒܚܙܪܐ ܠܗ̇
ܐܦ ܗܘ. ܡܕܡ ܕܝܢ ܕܠܘ

ܡܢ ܐܚܪ̈ܝܢ ܡܬܬܙܝܥ:
ܐܠܐ ܡܢ ܝܬܗ ܐܝܬ
ܠܗ ܙܘܥܬܐ ܐܝܟ ܢܦܫܐ
ܕܗܝ ܡܢ ܝܬܗ̇ ܡܬܬܙܝܥܐ.
ܠܐ ܡܬܚܘܐ ܠܦܓܪܐ
ܙܘܥܬܗ. ܢܦܫܐ ܗܝ ܓܝܪ
ܠܓܘ ܕܡܢ ܢܦܫܗ ܡܬܬܙܝܥ:
ܗܝ ܕܕܠܐ ܓܫܡܐ ܢܬܬܙܝܥ.
ܗܘ ܕܝܢ ܕܕܠܐ ܓܫܡܐ
ܡܬܬܙܝܥ. ܠܝܬ ܚܠܝܢܐ
ܠܘܚܡܗ. ܡܕܡ ܓܝܪ ܕܕܠܐ
ܓܫܡܐ ܗܘ. ܠܝܬ ܫܘܠܡܐ
ܠܘܚܡܗ. ܘܡܕܡ ܕܠܝܬ
ܫܘܠܡܐ ܠܘܚܡܗ ܠܐ
ܡܬܚܫܒ. ܘܡܕܡ ܕܠܐ
ܡܬܚܫܒ ܠܐ ܡܬܐܡܪ.
ܐܦ ܗܘ ܡܚܝܠ ܕܢܦܫܐ
ܡܢ ܝܬܗ̇ ܡܬܬܙܝܥܐ
fol. 142 b
ܐܝܟ ܕܫܘܝܢ. ܠܐ ܡܬܚܙܝܐ
ܡܫܠܐ ܠܗ̇. ܘܠܐ ܚܫܠܐ
ܡܕܘܕ ܠܗ. ܟܠ ܙܒܢ
ܗܟܝܠ ܐܝܕܐ ܕܡܢ
ܟܝܢܗ ܠܐ ܫܠܝܛ
ܟܠܗ ܚܘܫܒܐ ܠܐ
ܡܬܚܫܒܐ. ܟܝܢܐ ܓܝܪ
ܠܡܠܬܐ ܘܚܘܫܒܐ

ܗܝ. ܘܡܛܠ ܗܕܐ
ܡܬܚܫܒܢܘܬܐ ܗܝ.
ܦܓܪܐ ܗܟܝܠ ܡܢ ܟܝܢܗ
ܡܬܚܫܒ ܘܡܢ ܡܠܬܗ
ܡܬܚܙܐ. ܟܝܢܗ ܕܝܢ
ܐܬܚܙܝ. ܟܪ̈ܝܟܐ
ܘܟܘܪܗܢܐ ܘܡܟܘܬܐ.
ܠܟܝܢܗ ܕܝܢ ܫܘܦܪܐ
ܘܚܝܐ ܘܚܠܝܡܘܬܐ. ܐܦ
ܗܘ ܕܝܢ ܕܢܦܫܐ ܠܐ
ܡܢ ܟܝܢܗ ܡܬܝܕܥܐ:
ܘܠܐ ܡܢ ܟܝܢܗ ܡܫܬܪܪܐ:
ܟܝܢܗ ܐܬܚܙܝ:
ܕܚܠܝܘܬܐ ܘܫܘܦܪܐ:
ܘܠܠܝܘܬܐ ܘܕܐܝܟ ܗܠܝܢ:
ܟܝܢܗ ܕܝܢ ܕܕܡܘܬܐ
ܘܠܚܟܡܘܬܐ: ܘܢܨܝܚܘܬܐ
ܘܕܕ̈ܡܝܢ ܠܗܝܢ: ܗܠܝܢ
ܕܝܢ ܠܢܦܫܐ ܠܐ ܫܪ̈ܝܢ.
ܐܘ ܡܩܝܡܢ. ܡܕܡܟܐ
ܕܝܢ ܕܠܐ ܡܢܬܐ ܢܦܫܐ.
ܕܐܦ ܡܬܚܫܒܢܘܬܐ
ܗܝ ܢܦܫܐ ܀
ܕܡܬܚܫܒܢܘܬܐ ܐܝܬܝܗ̇
ܢܦܫ ܡܢ ܦܓܪ̈ܢܝܬܐ
ܐܝܟ ܫܘܐ. ܠܘܩܕܡ

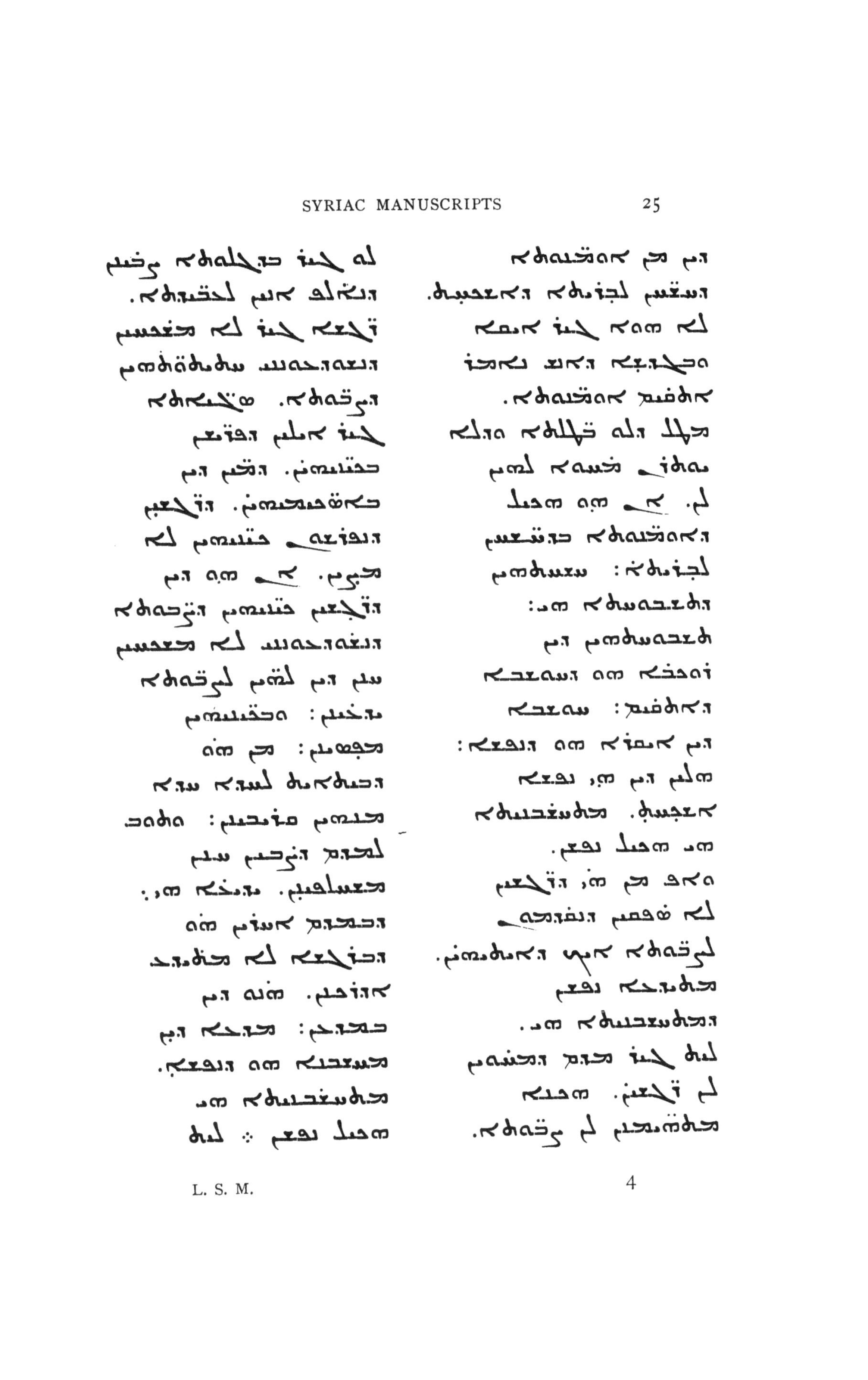

ܡܕܡ ܕܠܐ ܡܢ ܡܕܡ
ܕܢܒܕܘܢܗ̇ ܢܛܪܝܢ ܚܠܦ
ܠܗ. ܠܐ ܕܝܢ ܡܕܡ
ܐܚܪܝܢ ܐܝܬܘܗ̇ܝ ܗܢܐ.
ܐܠܐ ܙܒܢܘܬܗ̇ ܕܢܦܫܐ.
ܡܛܠ ܟܝܢ ܕܠܘ ܡܢ ܠܒܪ
ܡܬܝܗܒܐ ܠܗ̇ ܡܕܒܪܢܘܬܐ fol. 143 a
ܕܬܒܥܘܬܐ: ܐܠܐ ܗ̇ܝ
ܡܢ ܬܪܒܝܬܗ̇ ܡܬܝܠܕܐ.
ܡܛܠ ܗܢܐ ܦܘܩܕܢܐ
ܐܬܒܐ ܠܗ ܒܢܬܗ̇.

ܘܡܢ ܫܘܦܪܐ ܠܗ̇
ܠܚܒܪܐ. ܐܝܡܪܗ̇ ܕܝܢ
ܘܪܒܘܬܗ̇ ܕܢܦܫܐ ܗܘܝܐ.
ܕܒܝܫܘܬܐ ܥܠ ܝܕܘ
ܬܬܒܪ. ܒܗܕܐ ܗܘ
ܐܬܚܙܝܬ ܕܡܬܚܪܐ ܡܢ
ܙ̈ܢܝܐ. ܠܗܘܠܢܐ ܐܪܐ
ܐܝܬܝܗ̇ ܢܦܫܐ. ܗ̇ܝ
ܕܝܢ ܡܬܚܫܚܢܘܬܐ ܀
ܫܠܡ ܡܐܡܪܐ ܕܬܐܢܘ
ܠܦܝܠܘܣܘܦܐ: ܥܠ ܢܦܫܐ:

(11) The discourse of Theano is followed by Sayings of the Philosophers, and these are apparently the same collection as is found in Sachau, *Inedita*, pp. 66: after which follows:

ܬܘܒ ܫܪܒܐ ܕܚܟܝ̈ܡܐ fol. 145 a
ܦܠܣܘܦܘܣ ܐܡܪ. ܐܢܫܐ
ܕܗܝܡܢܐ ܠܗ ܕܠܡܕܡ
ܠܐ ܢܬܦܠܣܦ. ܬܘܒ
ܘܦܪ̈ܐ ܘܣܟ̈ܝܡܐ
ܘܡܕܘܒܐ: ܐܝܟ ܡܫܟܚܝܢ
ܕܢܦܫܘܢܝܗ̇ ܠܐ
ܡܬܦܠܣܦ. ܡܛܠ ܕܠܗܕܐ
ܗܘ ܐܬܦܠܣܦ ܗܘܐ.
ܕܦܢܫܐ ܠܐ ܢܦܠ.
ܕܗܘܘ ܠܗ ܗܢܘܢ ܡܬܪ̈ܐ
ܐܦ ܗܘ ܠܗܘܢ ܢܗܪܐ

ܡܛܠ ܕܠܘܬܗ̇. ܘܠܘ
ܡܛܠ ܕܠܐ ܐܬܦܠܣܦ
ܐܒܕܬ ܠܗ̇ ܚܟܡܬܐ
ܗܘܝܘ ܟܕ ܐܒܕ ܗܘܐ
ܡܢܗ̇. ܘܠܘ ܗܝ ܡܢܗ̇.
ܐܣܛܘܦܘ ܐܡܪ.
ܒܡܐܡܪ̈ܐ ܗ̇ܘ ܣܟܝܢܐ
ܘܒܡܫܡܥܐ. ܡܗܘܢܐ.
ܡܬܢܒܝܢ ܟ̈ܠܝܐ ܡܗܘܢ̈ܐ
ܕܢܦܫ̈ܬܐ. ܘܕܠܐ ܗܝܟܢ.
ܗ̇ܘܝܢ ܠܝ ܣ̈ܘܬܐ
ܕܠܐ ܦܘܪܢܝ. ܘܒܚܝܪܐ

ܕܠܐ ܡܢܝܐ ܒܗܘܢܐ.
ܘܐܡܝܢܐ ܕܠܐ ܡܫܚܫܢܐ
ܕܢܬܬܘܠ ܒܡܐܘܬܐ
ܥܘܦܐ ܚܘܠܢܐ. ܗܒܢܐ
ܠܐ ܡܫܚܫܢܐ ܕܢܬܬܦܠ
ܪܚܝܠܐ ܚܢܢܐ. ܗܘ
ܕܢܒܓ ܕܢܐܡܪ ܘܢܫܬܒܚ.
ܥܠ ܟܠ ܡܕܡ ܕܡܫܘܚܬܐ
ܘܡܬܬܡܠܠܐ ܐܝܬ
ܠܗ ܒܠܚܘܕ ܀
܀ ܐܘܣܦܘܠܝܦ ܐܡܪ. ܀
ܐܘ ܬܬܢܐ ܙܒܘ
ܥܙܒܝܢ ܡܕܡ ܩܒܠܐ
ܘܫܒܝܢܐ: ܒܢܝ ܕܠܐ
ܦܪܫܝܢ ܐܝܟ ܐܢܫ
ܗܘ ܕܡܬܠܒܟ ܠܒܢܝܢܐ
ܕܗܒܐ ܘܛܒܐ ܘܡܪܓܢܝܬܐ.
ܘܠܗ ܕܠܗ ܐܝܟ ܛܒܘܬܐ
ܗܘ ܚܫܒ ܠܗ: ܘܠܐ
ܗܘܐ ܐܝܟ ܗܘ ܕܡܕܡ
ܕܡܢܝܪ. ܒܠܚܘܕ ܝܕܥܬܐ
ܘܒܗܘܢܐ ܕܦܪܫܝܢ ܘܝܕܥܝܢ.
܀ ܢܐܣܛܘܦ ܐܡܪ. ܀
ܝܘܒܐ ܘܡܠܒܢܐ ܘܫܒܝܚܐ
ܘܪܫܐ ܘܡܕܒܪܢܐ.
ܕܐܡܪܝܢ ܘܡܠܦܝܢ

ܡܕܡ ܕܠܐ ܡܬܚܡܝܢ
ܠܗ ܒܟܝܢܗ. ܙܕܩ ܗܘ
ܕܢܬܒܣܪܘܢ ܒܠܝܐܝܬ.
ܘܢܬܫܒܚܘܢ ܒܐܢܐܝܬ:
ܕܐܡܪܝܢ ܡܕܡ ܕܠܐ
ܟܝܢܝܢ: ܘܪܓܝܢ ܘܡܫܒܚܝܢ
ܒܡܕܡ ܕܐܦ ܗܠܝܢ
ܒܣܪܝܢ ܒܗ. ܠܘ ܟܝܢܐ
ܒܗܝ ܕܐܡܪܝܢ ܡܕܡ
ܕܝܕܥܝܢ ܡܬܦܪܫܝܢ
ܫܒܝܚܐ. ܐܠܐ ܡܢ
ܗܝ ܕܟܝܢܝܢ ܘܡܢ ܐܡܪܝܢ:
ܡܬܡܪܝܢ ܦܪܘܫܐ ܘܝܕܘܥܐ.
ܘܟܠܝܢ ܬܦܢܘܢ ܘܠܐ
ܒܣܝܪܝܢ. ܡܢܐ ܕܬܒܟܝܢ
ܡܩܠܘܬܐ ܕܡܘܪܢܝܐ fol. 145 b
ܡܢ ܐܢܪܝܐ ܀ ܀
ܝܘܣܦ ܐܡܪ:
ܐܠܘ ܚܟܝܡܐ ܕܡܕܡܝܢ:
ܠܐ ܒܟܠܗ ܗܘܘ
ܘܐܪܡܝܘ ܠܗ ܗܝܐ
ܡܠܐܐ ܕܝܘܬܪܢܐ:
ܘܗܢܐ ܗܪܓܐ ܒܡܣܟܐ:
ܘܡܬܝܒܘ ܠܗ ܗܠܝܢ ܛܪܒܐ
ܫܒܬܐ ܕܝܩܘܡ ܒܗܘܢ:
ܘܕܪܫܘ ܠܗ ܗܠܝܢ

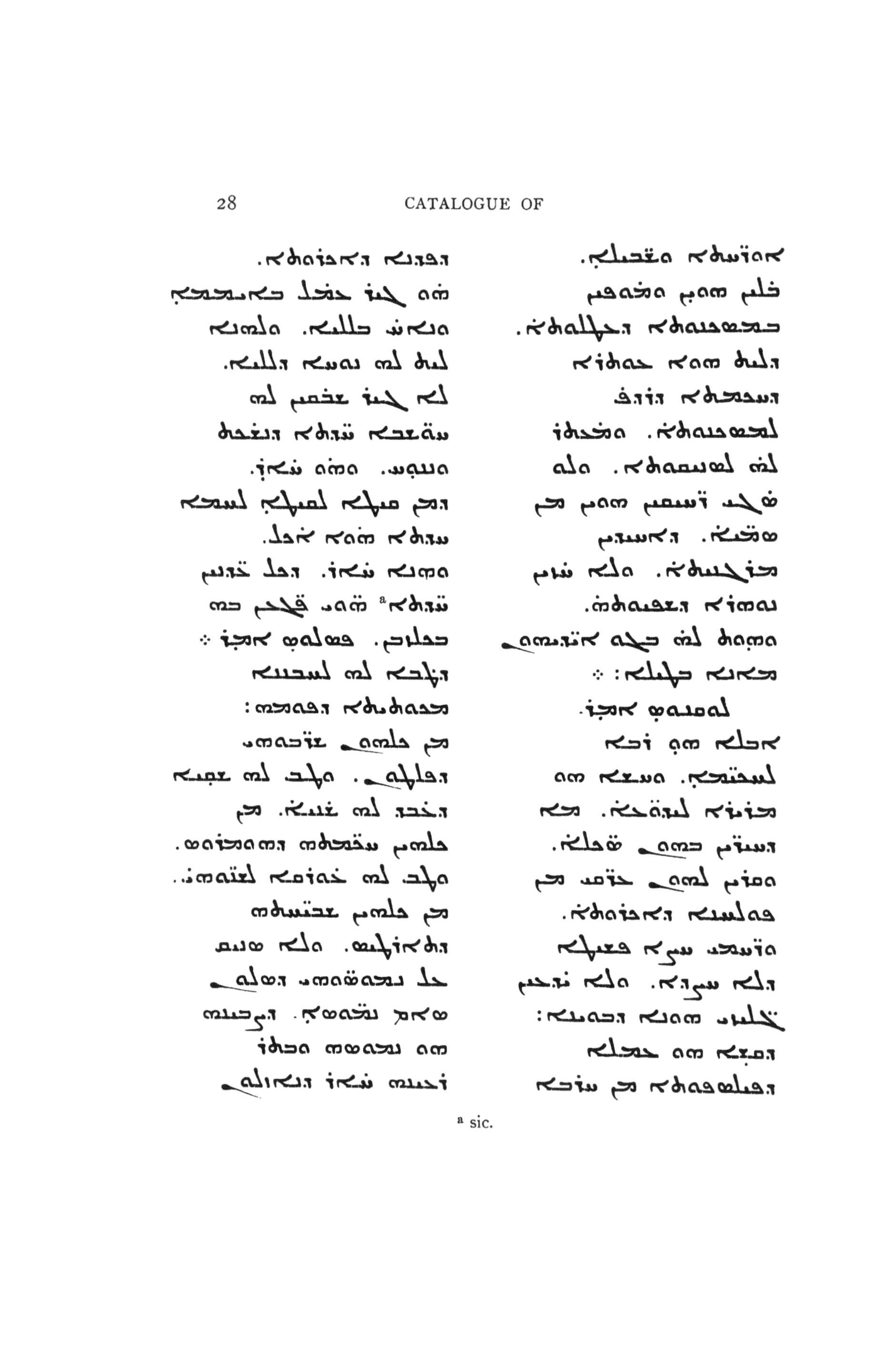

fol.
146 a

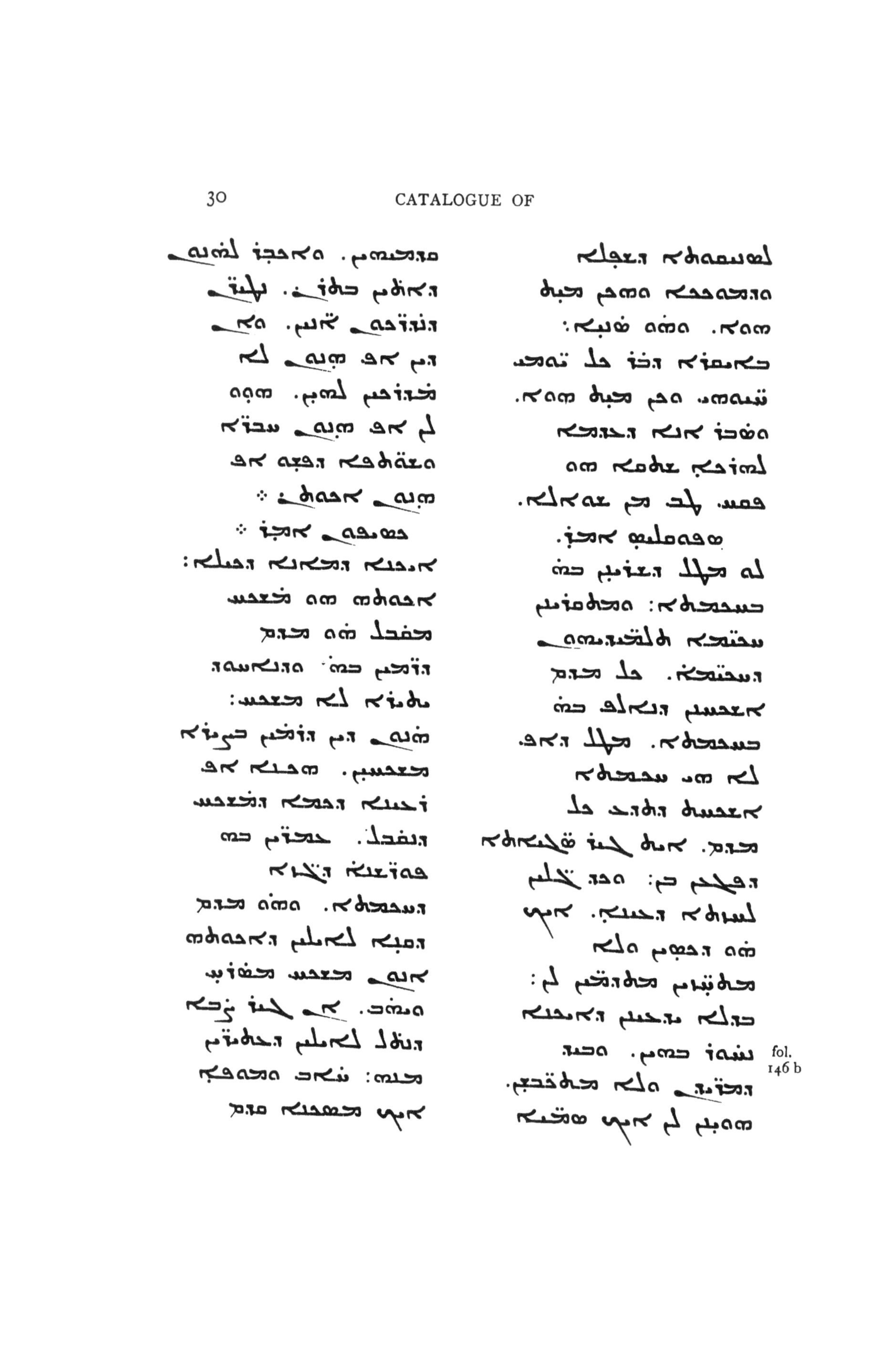

 [a]
 [fol. 147 a]
 [fol. 147 a]

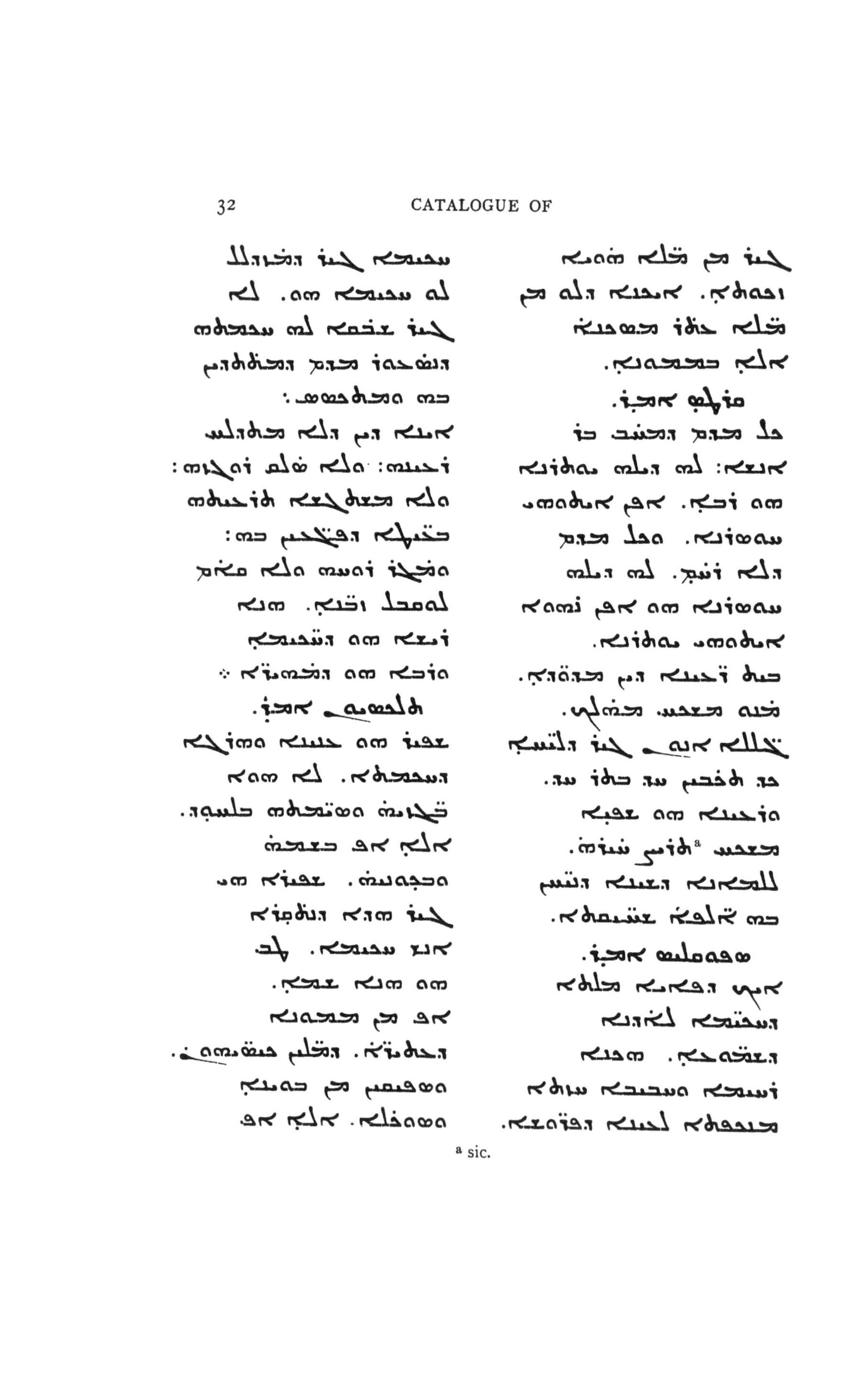

[a].

لا محمد دهم محمد ملامحة
معمد للا محمد دهمحمد.
ومحمد محدة الملحم محمد. ودم محمد
هم هجلم محمد. ماحم محمد. لحم
هم محمد. هم محمد. لحم
محمد محملا لحم. محمد حجمحة
معمد محمد ملامحة.

دمحمد حمد محمد لحم محمد
دمحمد محمد حجلم. محمد
ملل دلقحلحم محمد. وحم
محمد لمحم محمد. محمد
لحم دمحم دمحملا: حمد
حمد لحم دمحمد ومحمد. ملحم
دمحلا محملا محمد. محمد
لحم دمحمد. محمد
محمد هم لحم محملا.
دمحمد لحم: ملحم لحم
دمحمد دمحمد لحم.
محمد لحم حجحم
ومحمد محملا للمحمد.
محمد محمد لدمحم:
محمد محمد دمحم
محمد محمد دمحمد محمد
محمد لمحم محمد
دمحمد. حمد ملحم
محمد لحم حمد. حمد ملحم

fol.
147 b

fol.
148 a

fol.
148 b

5—2

fol.
149 a

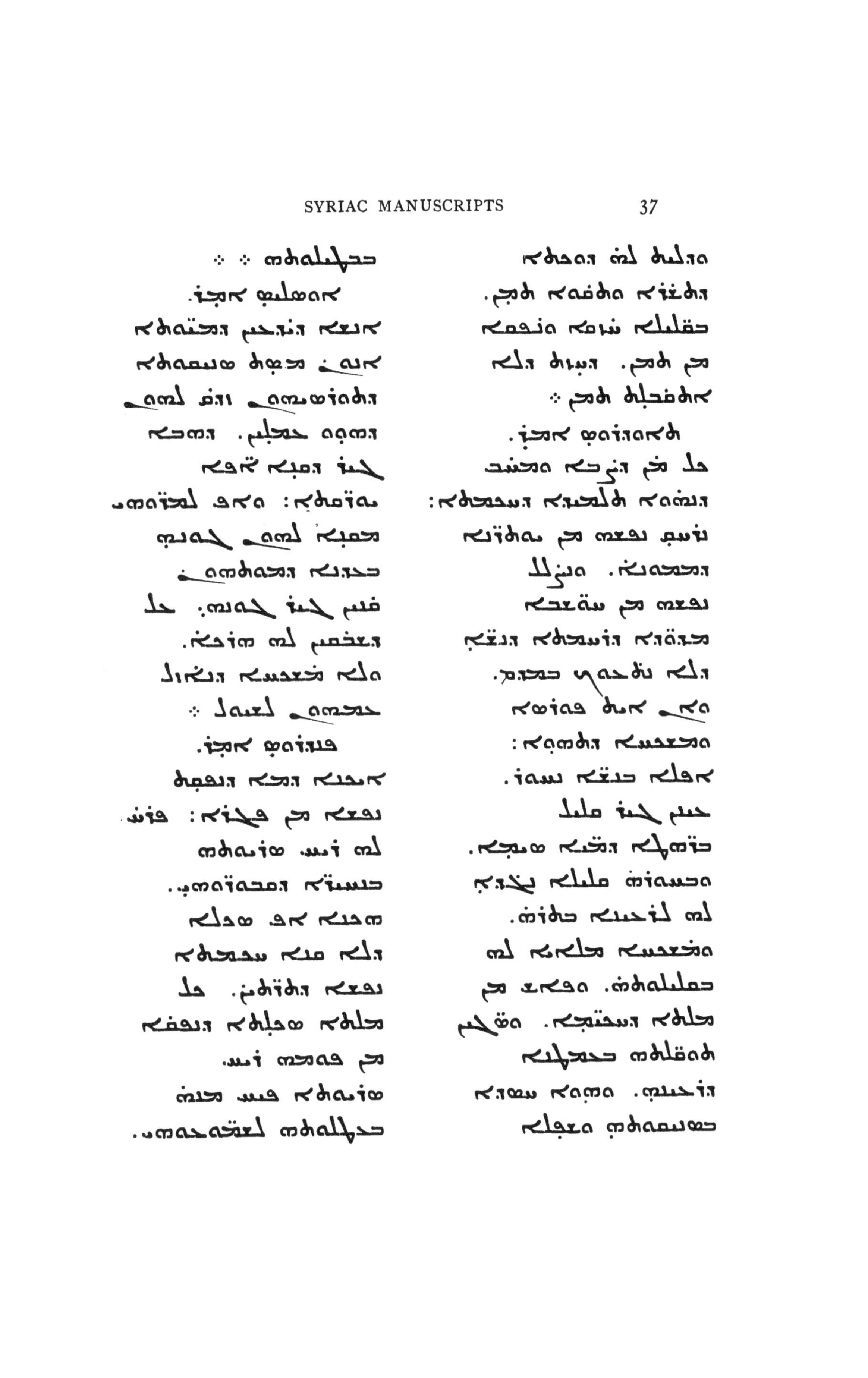

   fol.
149 b

---

(12) A commentary on Ecclesiastes by Mar John the Anchorite, fol. 151—214. (13) Commentaries of Chrysostom on Matthew, fol. 214 ad finem.

Vellum; one column till fol. 93; two columns from fol. 93 till the end; Estrangelo; seventh century.

17

Τὰ Εὐαγγέλια, αἱ Πράξεις· αἱ Καθολικαὶ Ἐπιστολαὶ καὶ αἱ τοῦ Ἁγίου Παύλου.

Σημειώσεις συναρμοσθεῖσαι ὑπὸ τὰ Εὐαγγέλια.

μεμβράνη· κγ′ × ιε′· φύλλα ρνζ′ καὶ πρόσθετα ε′· δίστη-λον· γραμμαὶ λθ′· στρογγύλη γραφή· τοῦ ἐννάτου αἰῶνος.

The Gospels, Acts, Catholic Epistles and Pauline Epistles.

Harmonised References at the foot of the Gospels.

Vellum ; 23 × 15 ; 157 leaves and five added ; two columns; 39 lines; Estrangelo; ninth century.

18

Ἀναγνώσματά τινα περὶ ἀκολουθιῶν· ἐλλειπὲς τὴν ἀρχὴν καὶ τὸ τέλος.

μεμβράνη· κδ′ × ιη′· φύλλα σμ′· μονόστηλον· γραμμαὶ κδ′· στρογγύλη γραφή.

Lections and liturgical matter, incomplete at the beginning and end.

Vellum ; 24 × 18 ; 240 leaves ; one column ; 24 lines ; Estrangelo.

19

Τόμος ὁμιλιῶν· ἐλλειπὴς τὴν ἀρχὴν καὶ τὸ τέλος· ἐλλει-πὴς τὸ δέσιμον·

Περιέχει σχόλιά τινα περὶ τοῦ Ἄσματος Ἀσμάτων· λήγει εἰς τὴν δεκάτην τρίτην ὁμιλίαν.

μεμβράνη· κϛ′ × ιζ′· φύλλα ξβ′· δίστηλον· γραμμαὶ κθ′· στρογγύλη γραφή.

A volume of homilies on the Song of Songs, imperfect at the beginning and end, and without binding.

The head-line is ᕁᲂᏅᏋᏬᏑᎣ ᕁᲂᏅᏋᏬᏑᎣ; it ends with
the thirteenth homily.

Vellum; 26 × 17; 62 leaves; two columns; 29 lines;
Estrangelo.

20

Ἀναγνώσματα διὰ τὸ ἔτος· μεμβράνη· κα΄ × κ΄· φύλλα
ρπγ΄· δίστηλον· γραμμαὶ κα΄· τοῦ δωδεκάτου αἰῶνος.

ἐλλειπὲς τὴν ἀρχὴν δύο φύλλων.

Lections for the year; vellum; 21 × 20; 183 leaves;
two columns; 21 lines; twelfth century.

Two leaves lost at the beginning.

21

Εὐαγγέλια κατ᾽ ἀναγνώσεις καὶ λειτουργικά τινα· ἐλλειπὲς τὴν ἀρχὴν καὶ τὸ τέλος.

μεμβράνη· ι΄ × η΄· φύλλα σνδ΄· δίστηλον· γραμμαὶ κγ΄.

Lectionary and liturgical matter, imperfect at the
beginning and end.

Vellum; 10 × 8; 254 leaves; two columns; 23 lines.

22

Εὐαγγέλιον κατ᾽ ἀναγνώσεις καὶ λειτουργικά τινα· ἐλλειπὲς τὴν ἀρχὴν καὶ τὸ τέλος.

μεμβράνη· κζ΄ × ιη΄· φύλλα ρξε΄· μονόστηλον· γραμμαὶ
κη΄.

Lectionary and liturgical matter, imperfect at the
beginning and end.

Vellum; 27 × 18; 165 leaves; one column; 28 lines.

23

ᕁᲂᏑᏓᎣ ᕁᲂᏴᏑᎣᏑᏭ Βιβλίον τῶν ἀναχωριτῶν τῶν
αἰγυπτιακῶν· ἐλλειπὲς τὴν ἀρχὴν καὶ τὸ τέλος.

μεμβράνη· κε΄ × ιθ΄· φύλλα ρκα΄· δίστηλον· γραμμαὶ λδ΄· στρογγύλη γραφή· τοῦ ἐννάτου αἰῶνος.

The Book of the Egyptian Solitaries; imperfect at the beginning and end.

Vellum; 25 × 19; 121 leaves; two columns; 34 lines; Estrangelo; ninth century.

24

Τὰ ἔργα τοῦ Μὰρ Ἰσαάκ, ἔλλειπὲς τὴν ἀρχήν· μετ' ἀποσπασμάτων περὶ τῆς ἱστορίας τῶν Πατέρων τῆς Ἐρήμου, Διονυσίου τοῦ Τελλ-Μὰρ κ.τ.λ.

μεμβράνη· κε΄ × ιθ΄· φύλλα σκα΄· δίστηλον· γραμμαὶ κζ΄· στρογγύλη γραφή· δεκάτου αἰῶνος.

The works of Mar Isaac, imperfect at the beginning; also extracts from the story of the Fathers of the Desert, Dionysius of Tell-Mar etc.

Vellum; 25 × 19; 221 leaves; two columns; 27 lines; Estrangelo; tenth century.

25

Λειτουργία· μεμβράνη· κ΄ × ιε΄· φύλλα σνε΄· μονόστηλον· γραμμαὶ κ΄· στρογγύλη γραφή· νεωτέρας ἐποχῆς.

Liturgy; vellum; 20 × 15; 255 leaves; one column; 20 lines; Estrangelo; late.

26

Τὰ τοῦ Μὰρ Ἠσαΐου συγγράμματα· ἀκολουθεῖ ἀπόσπασμα ἀπὸ τοῦ Χρυσοστόμου, καὶ σύντομος βίος τοῦ Ἀποστόλου Ἰωάννου.

μεμβράνη· κθ΄ × ιε΄· φύλλα ρνϛ΄· μονόστηλον· γραμμαὶ λ΄· στρογγύλη γραφή· ἐννάτου αἰῶνος.

The writings of Mar Isaiah, followed by an extract from Chrysostom and a short life of the Apostle John.

Vellum; 29 × 15; 156 leaves; one column; 30 lines; Estrangelo; ninth century.

27

Τροπάριον μετὰ πολλῶν σελίδων παλιμψήστων, ἑλληνικῶν τε καὶ συριακῶν. Τὰ μὲν ἑλληνικὰ τροπάριόν ἐστι, τὰ
δὲ συριακὰ κείμενόν τι ἐκ τῆς Παλαιᾶς Διαθήκης. Εἰς τὸ
τέλος εἰσ Palimpsest of Old Syriac Gospels. No. 30ῆς μαρτυρίας
τῆς Ἁγί.   . . LUKE VII. 39—VIII. 2.

μεμβράνη· κδ´ × ις´· φύλλα ριζ´· μονόστηλον· γραμμαὶ
κζ´· τρισκαιδεκάτου αἰῶνος.

A Troparion, with many pages palimpsest in Greek and
Syriac; the Greek being a troparion and the Syriac a text
of the Old Testament. At the end are some leaves of Mar
Ephraim and the martyrdom of St Barbara.

Vellum; 24 × 16; 117 leaves; one column; 27 lines;
thirteenth century.

28

Τὸ τῶν Βασιλέων Βιβλίον· ἐλλειπὲς τὴν ἀρχὴν καὶ τὸ
τέλος· χωρὶς δεσίμου.

μεμβράνη· κε´ × ις´· φύλλα Ϟγ´· μονόστηλον· γραμμαὶ
κ´· στρογγύλη γραφή· ὀγδόου αἰῶνος.

The Book of Kings; imperfect at the beginning and
end; without covers.

Vellum; 25 × 16; 93 leaves; one column; 20 lines;
Estrangelo; eighth century.

29

Ὁμιλίαι τοῦ Μὰρ Ἰακώβου· τοῦ Μὰρ Ἰωάννου· τοῦ
Μὰρ Ἰσαάκ· κ.τ.λ.

μεμβράνη· κε´ × ιδ´· φύλλα πβ´· δίστηλον· γραμμαὶ μγ´·
στρογγύλη γραφή.

Homilies of Mar Jacob; Mar John; Mar Isaac, etc.

Vellum; 25 × 14; 82 leaves; 2 columns; 43 lines.
Estrangelo.

PLATE III.

Palimpsest of Old Syriac Gospels.　No. 30.

LUKE VII. 39—VIII. 2.

To face page 43.

30

Παλίμψηστον· οὗ τὸ ἄνω κείμενόν ἐστι

Μαρτυρολογία ἢ Ἐκλεκταὶ Βιογραφίαι Ἁγίων Γυναικῶν ὑπὸ Ἰωάννου τοῦ Ἀναχωρητοῦ. Ὁ πρόλογός ἐστι·

Palimpsest. The upper writing is:

A martyrology.

ܒܚܝܠܗ ܕܡܪܢ. ܝܫܘܥ: ܡܫܝܚܐ: [ܒܪ]ܗ:
ܕܐܠܗܐ: ܚܝܐ: ܡܫܪܐ: ܐܢܐ....ܐ ܚܛܝܐ:
ܝܘܚܢܢ: ܚܒܝܫܐ: ܕܒܝܬ ܡܪܝ: ܘܟܬܒ: ܕܐܬܚܘܒ:
ܬܫܥܝܬܐ ܡܓܒܝܬܐ: ܘܥܠ ܢܫܐ ܩܕܝܫܬܐ:
ܘܡܛܐܬ: ܒܟܬܒܐ: ܠܛܘܒܢܝܬܐ ܡܪܬܐ ܬܩܠܐ
ܬܠܡܝܕܬܗ ܕܦܘܠܘܣ: ܫܠܝܚܐ: ܛܘܒܢܐ....

Βοηθείᾳ τοῦ Κυρίου ἡμῶν Ἰησοῦ Χριστοῦ [υἱοῦ] θεοῦ ζῶντος ἄρχομαι (ἐγὼ) ὁ ἁμαρτωλός, Ἰωάννης ὁ ἀναχωρητὴς Ἁγίας Βεθ-μαρι, γράφειν Ἱστορίας Ἐκλεκτὰς περὶ Ἁγίων Γυναικῶν. πρῶτον, τὰ γραφέντα περὶ τῆς Μακαρίτιδος Κυρίας Θέκλης μαθητρίας Παύλου, τοῦ μακαρίτου Ἀποστόλου. φύλ. α'—κα'.

The prologue is:

By the strength of our Lord Jesus Christ, [the Son] of the Living God, I begin, [I] the sinner, John the Recluse of St Beth-Mari, to write Select Narratives about holy women. First, the writings about our Blessed Lady Thecla, disciple of Paul the Blessed Apostle. fol. 1—21.

περιέχει ἐπίσης·

ܘܕܘܒܪܗ̇: ܘܣܗܕܘܬܗ̇ ܕܛܘܒܢܝܬܐ ܐܘܓܢܝܐ
ܘܕ[ܐ]ܒܘܗ̇ ܦܝܠܝܦܘܣ ܘܕܥܠܝܗܘܢ ܕܐܣܗܕܘ ܥܡܗܘܢ

Αἱ Πράξεις καὶ ἡ Μαρτυρία τῆς Μακαρίτιδος Εὐγενείας καὶ τοῦ πατρός της Φιλίππου, καὶ περὶ τῶν συμμαρτυρούντων αὐτοῖς. φύλ. κα'—νβ'.

The Acts and Martyrdom of the Blessed Eugenia, and

of her father Philip, and of those who were martyred with them. fol. 21—52.

ܬܫܥܝܬܐ ܕܕܘܒܪ̈ܐ ܡܝܬܪ̈ܐ ܕܬܠܡܝܕܘܬܗ ܕܦܠܓܝܐ
ܙܢܝܬܐ ܕܡܢ ܐܢܛܝܘܟܝܐ ܡܕܝܢܬܐ ܕܣܘܪܝܐ:

Ἱστορία τῶν πράξεων τῶν ἐναρέτων τῆς μαθητεύσεως Πελαγίας τῆς πόρνης, ἀπ' Ἀντιοχείας, πόλεως Συρίας. φύλ. νγ'—ξθ'.

The story of the virtuous acts of the discipleship of Pelagia the harlot, of Antioch, a city of Syria. fol. 53—69.

ܬܘܒ: ܬܫܥܝܬܐ ܕܛܘܒܢܝܬܐ ܡܪܝܡ ܕܐܬܩܪܝܬ
ܡܪܝܢܘܣ: ·

Πάλιν· ἡ ἱστορία τῆς Μακαρίτιδος Μαρίας, ἥτις ὀνομάζεται Μαρῖνος. φύλ. ξθ'—οϛ'.

Again, the story of the Blessed Mary, who is called Marinus. fol. 69—76.

ܬܘܒ: ܬܫܥܝܬܐ ܕܐܦܪܘܣܘܢܝܐ ܒܐܠܟܣܢܕܪܝܐ:

Πάλιν· ἡ ἱστορία τῆς Εὐφροσύνης ἐν Ἀλεξανδρείᾳ. φύλ. οϛ'—πδ'.

Again, the story of Euphrosyne in Alexandria. fol. 76—84.

ܬܫܥܝܬܐ ܬܘܒ ܕܛܘܒܢܝܬܐ ܐܢܝܣܝܡܘܣ:

Ἡ ἱστορία πάλιν τῆς Μακαρίτιδος Ὀνησίμου. φύλ. πδ'—ϙβ'.

The story, again, of the Blessed Onesimus. fol. 84—92.

ܬܘܒ: ܣܗܕܘܬܐ ܕܩܕܝܫܬܐ ܕܪܘܣܝܣ ܘܕܐܝܠܝܢ
ܕܣܗܕܘ ܥܡܗ ܒܐܢܛܝܘܟܝܐ:

Πάλιν ἡ μαρτυρία τῆς Ἁγίας Δρύσις καὶ τῶν συμμαρτυρηθέντων αὐτῇ ἐν Ἀντιοχείᾳ. φύλ. ϙβ'—ϙε'.

Again, the martyrdom of St Drusis, and of those who witnessed with her at Antioch. fol. 92—95.

ܬܘܒ: ܬܫܥܝܬܐ ܕܩܕܝܫܬܐ ܒܪܒܪܐ ܒܡܕܝܢܬܐ
ܫܡܫܐ:

Πάλιν· ἡ ἱστορία τῆς Ἁγίας Βαρβάρης ἐν Ἡλιοπόλει. φύλ. Ϟε΄—ρ΄.

Again, the story of St Barbara in Heliopolis. fol. 95—100.

: ܐܣܛܪܘܢ ܕܒܪܬܐ ܛܘܒܢܝܬܐ

Ἡ μαρτυρία τῆς Μακαρίτιδος Μαρίας. φύλ. ρ΄—ρε΄.
The martyrdom of the Blessed Mary. fol. 100—105.

ܬܘܒ: ܬܫܥܝܬܐ ܕܐܝܪܝܢܝ ܩܕܝܫܬܐ:

Πάλιν· ἡ ἱστορία τῆς Ἁγίας Εἰρήνης. φύλ. ρε΄—ρλζ΄.
Again, the story of St Irene. fol. 105—137.

ܬܘܒ: ܣܗܕܘܬܐ ܕܐܘܦܡܝܐ ܛܘܒܢܝܬܐ ܗܘܬ
ܥܠ ܡܝܠܐ ܩܪܝܒܐ ܠܩܠܩܕܘܢܐ ܡܕܝܢܬܐ ܟܕ ܐܡܠܟ
ܐܘܛܩܪܛܘܪ ܩܣܪ ܛܪܘܢܐ: ܡܢ

Πάλιν· ἡ μαρτυρία τῆς Μακαρίτιδος Εὐφημίας, ἥτις ἐγένετο ἐπὶ τοῦ μιλιοδείκτου πλησίον εἰς Χαλκηδῶνα τὴν πόλιν, βασιλεύοντος τοῦ Αὐτοκράτορος Καίσαρου τοῦ τυράννου. φύλ. ρλζ΄—ρμθ΄.

Again, the martyrdom of the Blessed Euphemia, which took place by the mile-stone out of the city of Chalcedon, in the days of the Emperor, the tyrant Cæsar. fol. 137—149.

ܬܘܒ: ܣܗܕܘܬܐ ܕܣܘܦܝܐ ܘܕܬܠܬ ܒܢܬܗ
ܒܬܘܠܬܐ: ܦܝܣܛܝܣ: ܗܠܦܝܣ: ܘܐܓܦܐ:

Πάλιν· ἡ μαρτυρία Σοφίας καὶ τῶν τριῶν αὐτῆς θυγατέρων παρθένων Πίστεως, Ἐλπίδος, καὶ Ἀγάπης. φύλ. ρν΄—ρξα΄.

Again, the martyrdom of Sophia and of her three daughters, virgins, Pistis, Elpis, and Agape. fol. 150—161.

ܬܘܒ: ܣܗܕܘܬܐ: ܕܬܐܕܣܝܐ: ܒܬܘܠܬܐ:

Πάλιν, ἡ μαρτυρία Θεοδοσίας τῆς παρθένου. φύλ. ρξ΄—ρξα΄.

Again, the martyrdom of Theodosia the virgin. fol. 160—161.

ܬܘܒ: ܣܗܕܘܬܐ ܕܬܐܕܣܝܐ ܒܬܘܠܬܐ:

Πάλιν· ἡ μαρτυρία Θεοδότης τῆς πόρνης. φύλ. ρξα΄—ρξγ΄.

Again, the martyrdom of Theodota the harlot. fol. 161—163.

ܬܘܒ: ܡܦܩ ܒܪܘܚܐ ܕܥܠ ܗܝ ܡܢ ܗܝܡܢܘܬܐ:

Πάλιν, ἀπολογία ὑπὲρ τῆς πίστεως. φύλ. ρξγ΄—ρξε΄.
Again, an Apology for the faith. fol. 163—165.

ܬܘܒ: ܟܬܒܝܢ ܬܫܥܝܬܐ ܕܫܘܫܢ:

Πάλιν, γράφομεν τὴν ἱστορίαν Σουσάννης. φύλ. ρξε΄—ρο΄.

Again, we write the story of Susanna. fol. 165—170.

ܬܘܒ: ܣܗܕܘܬܐ ܕܩܘܦܪܝܢܘܣ ܚܪܫܐ ܘܝܘܣܛܐ ܒܬܘܠܬܐ:

Πάλιν· ἡ μαρτυρία Κυπριάνου τοῦ μάγου καὶ Ἰούστης τῆς παρθένου. φύλ. ρο΄—ρπ΄.

Again, the martyrdom of Cyprian the wizard and Justa the virgin. fol. 170—180.

ܬܘܒ: ܡܐܡܪܐ ܕܡܪܝ ܐܦܪܝܡ ܕܝܪܬܐ ܕܦܪܕܝܣܐ.

Πάλιν, ὁμιλία τοῦ Μὰρ Ἐφραίμ, αἱ Μοναὶ τοῦ Παραδείσου. φύλ. ρπ΄—ρπα΄.

Again, a metrical homily of Mar Ephraim, the mansions of Paradise. fol. 180—181.

Τὸ δὲ κείμενον τοῦ παλιμψήστου ἐστὶν ὡς ἐξῆς

α΄. Τὰ τέσσαρα Εὐαγγέλια συριστὶ γεγραμμένα. φύλ. α΄—ρμ· ρμγ΄· ρμη΄.

β′. Συριακὰ ἀπόκρυφα, δηλαδὴ αἱ Πράξεις τοῦ Θωμᾶ καὶ ἡ Κοίμησις τῆς Παναγίας. φύλ. ρμα΄· ρμε΄· ρμϛ΄· ρν— ρο΄.

γ′. Ἑλληνικὸν Εὐαγγέλιον. ρμβ΄· ρμδ΄· ρμζ΄· ρμθ΄.

δ′. Ἑλληνικὸν κείμενόν τι. ροα΄—ρπβ΄.

The contents of the palimpsest are as follows:

I.   The four Gospels in Old Syriac.   fol. 1 to 140, 143, 148.

II.   Syriac Apocrypha, the Acts of Thomas, and the Repose of Mary.   fol. 141, 145, 146, 150 to 170.

III.   A text of the Gospel in Greek uncials.   142, 144, 147, 149.

IV.   A Greek text in sloping uncials.   171—182.

μεμβράνη. φύλλα ρπβ΄. κβ΄ × ιϛ΄.

τὸ νεώτερον κείμενόν ἐστι μονόστηλον. ἡ σελὶς ἔχει γραμμὰς κϛ΄. χρονολογεῖται τὸ ἔτος ψοη΄ μ. Χ.

τὸ ἀρχαιότερον πολύτιμον κείμενόν ἐστι δίστηλον, ἀνώμαλον τὰς γραμμάς. Ἡ χρονολογία ἐστὶ δυσανάγνωστος.

Vellum.   182 leaves;   22 × 16.

The later text is in one column, with 26 lines in the page; date A.D. 778.

The more ancient under-writing is in two columns, with an irregular number of lines.   The date is illegible.

31

Ὁμιλίαι τοῦ Μὰρ Ἰωάννου· Μὰρ Ἰακώβου· κ.τ.λ.   μεμβράνη· ἐλλειπὲς τὴν ἀρχὴν καὶ τὸ τέλος· κε΄ × ιε΄· φύλλα ᾳ᾿; δίστηλον· γραμμαὶ λη΄.

Homilies of Mar John; Mar Jacob etc.; vellum; imperfect at the beginning and end; 25 × 15; 90 leaves; two columns; 38 lines.

32

Εὐαγγέλια κατ᾽ ἀναγνώσεις καὶ Προσευχαί· μεμβράνη· ιη΄ × ιγ΄· φύλλα ρλζ΄· μονόστηλον· γραμμαὶ κβ΄.

Lectionary and prayers; vellum; 18 × 13; 137 leaves; one column; 22 lines.

33

Σύντομα ἀποσπάσματα ἐκ τῶν Ἁγίων Γραφῶν· μετὰ συνεχῶν σχολίων· ἐλλειπὲς τὴν ἀρχὴν καὶ τὸ τέλος· κ΄ × ιδ΄· φύλλα ροζ΄· μονόστηλον· γραμμαὶ ιδ΄.

Short passages of Scripture; with continuous expository notes; imperfect at the beginning and end; 20 × 14; 177 leaves; one column; 14 lines.

34

35

Τὸ πρῶτον βιβλίον Σαμουήλ· μεμβράνη· κα΄ × ιγ΄· φύλλα ρθ΄· μονόστηλον· γραμμαὶ κγ΄· στρογγύλη γραφή· ἀρχαῖον.

The first book of Samuel; vellum; 21 × 13; 109 leaves; one column; 23 lines; Estrangelo; early.

36

Λειτουργία· μεμβράνη· ιγ΄ × λα΄· φύλλα ρη΄· μονόστηλον· γραμμαὶ ιε΄· νεωτέρας ἐποχῆς.

Service-book; vellum; 13 × 31; 108 leaves; one column; 15 lines; very late.

37

38

Μὰρ Ἡσαίας· ἐλλειπὲς τὴν ἀρχήν· μεμβράνη· κδ′ × ιζ′· φύλλα κθ′· μονόστηλον· γραμμαὶ λγ′· τῆς ι′ ἑκατονταετηρίδος.

Mar Isaiah; imperfect at the beginning; vellum; 24 × 17; 29 leaves; one column; 33 lines; tenth century.

39

Ἀκολουθία μετὰ παλιμψήστου συριακοῦ· μεμβράνη· ις′ × ια′· φύλλα σκε′· μονόστηλον· γραμμαὶ ις′· νεωτέρας ἐποχῆς.

A service-book with Syriac palimpsest; vellum; 16 × 11; 225 leaves; one column; 16 lines; very late.

40

Εἱρμολόγιον· ιβ′ × θ′· φύλλα ρξε′· γραμμαὶ ιδ′· μεμβράνη.

Hirmologion; 12 × 9; 165 leaves; 14 lines; vellum.

41

Ψαλτήριον· μεμβράνη· ιγ′ × θ′· φύλλα ν′· μονόστηλον· γραμμαὶ κε′· στρογγύλη γραφή.

Psalter; vellum; 13 × 9; 50 leaves; one column; 25 lines; Estrangelo.

42

Εὐχολόγιον· μεμβράνη καὶ χάρτης· ις′ × ι′· φύλλα σξθ′· γραμμαὶ ιδ′· νεωτέρας ἐποχῆς.

Prayers; vellum and paper; 16 × 10; 269 leaves; 14 lines; late.

43

Ψαλτήριον· μεμβράνη· ιη΄ × ιδ΄· φύλλα πϛ΄· ὧν τρία
ἄγραφα· γραμμαὶ ιζ΄· νεωτέρας ἐποχῆς.

Psalter; vellum; 18 × 14; 86 pages (3 blank); 17 lines;
late.

44

45

'Ακολουθία μετ' ἀναγνώσεων· ἐλλειπὲς τὴν ἀρχήν· μεμ-
βράνη· κζ΄ × κα΄· φύλλα ρλγ΄· δίστηλον· γραμμαὶ κβ΄.

Service-book with lections; imperfect at the beginning;
vellum; 27 × 21; 133 leaves; two columns; 22 lines.

46

Τὸ Βιβλίον τῶν Αἰγυπτιακῶν Πατέρων· ἐλλειπὲς τὴν
ἀρχὴν καὶ τὸ τέλος· μεμβράνη· κδ΄ × ιϛ΄· φύλλα ρη΄· δίστηλον·
γραμμαὶ λγ΄· στρογγύλη γραφή· τῆς θ΄ ἑκατονταετηρίδος.

The Book of the Egyptian Fathers; imperfect at the
beginning and end; vellum; 24 × 16; 108 leaves; two
columns; 33 lines; Estrangelo; ninth century.

47

48

Στιχεράριον· μεμβράνη· στρογγύλη γραφή· κγ΄ × ιδ΄·
φύλλα τκε΄· μονόστηλον· γραμμαὶ κε΄· νεωτέρας ἐποχῆς.

Sticherarion; vellum; Estrangelo; 23 × 14; 325 leaves;
one column; 25 lines; late.

49

50

Στιχεράριον· μεμβράνη· κα΄ × ιε΄· φύλλα Ϙη΄· μονόστη-
λον· γραμμαὶ ιθ΄· νεωτέρας ἐποχῆς.

Sticherarion; vellum; 21 × 15; 98 leaves; one column; 19 lines; late.

51

52

Τὰ ἔργα Διονυσίου τοῦ Ἀρειοπαγίτου· μεμβράνη· κ΄ × ιθ΄· φύλλα ριη΄· δίστηλον· γραμμαὶ λϛ΄· τῆς ζ΄ ἑκατονταετηρίδος· στρογγύλη γραφή.

The works of Dionysius the Areopagite; vellum; Estrangelo; 20 × 19; 118 leaves; two columns; 36 lines; seventh century.

53

54

Τὰ Εὐαγγέλια· αἱ Πράξεις· αἱ Καθολικαὶ Ἐπιστολαί· καὶ αἱ τοῦ Ἁγίου Παύλου· πͅριέχει φύλλα τινὰ ἀραβικὰ προτιθέντα· μεμβράνη· κδ΄ × ιϛ΄· φύλλα ρξθ΄· δέκα φύλλα μονόστηλα· ἔπειτα δίστηλον· στρογγύλη γραφή· τῆς η΄ ἑκατονταετηρίδος.

The Gospels, Acts, Catholic and Pauline Epistles; some leaves of Arabic prefixed; vellum; 24 × 16; 169 leaves; one column for 10 leaves; then two columns; Estrangelo; eighth century.

55

56

Λόγοι τοῦ Ἁγίου Ἰωάννου Κλίμακος· μεμβράνη· ἐλλειπὲς τὴν ἀρχὴν καὶ τὸ τέλος· ἀκολουθέντες δι' ὁμιλιῶν τινῶν
τοῦ Μὰρ Ἰακώβου καὶ Ἀναστασίου τῆς Ἀντιοχείας.

κδ' × ιε'· φύλλα πθ'· μονόστηλον· γραμμαὶ κη'· στρογγύλη γραφή· τῆς η' ἑκατονταετηρίδος.

St John Klimax; vellum; imperfect at the beginning
and end; and supplemented by homilies of Mar Jacob, and
Anastasius of Antioch.

24 × 15; 89 leaves; one column; 28 lines; Estrangelo;
eighth century.

57

58

Μὰρ Ἡσαίας· μεμβράνη· κδ' × ιϛ'· φύλλα κθ'· μονόστηλον·
γραμμαὶ λε'· τῆς η' ἑκατονταετηρίδος.

Mar Isaiah; vellum; 24 × 16; 29 leaves; one column;
35 lines; eighth century.

59

Ὁμιλίαι περὶ τοῦ Εὐαγγελίου Ἰωάννου· μεμβράνη·
ἐλλειπές· ἡ ὁμιλία ἡ ξγ' ἄρχει

ܪܬܠܐ ܡܢ ܝܘܚ ܕܝܘܢܩܪܣܘܡܘܣ

κϛ' × ιε'· φύλλα νη'· δίστηλον· γραμμαὶ λη'· τῆς θ' ἑκατον-
ταετηρίδος· στρογγύλη γραφή.

Homilies on St John; vellum; imperfect; 26 × 15;
58 leaves; two columns; 38 lines; ninth century; Estrangelo. We identify the text as that of Chrysostom.

60

Ὁμιλίαι τοῦ Εὐαγρίου· μεμβράνη· ἐλλειπὲς τὴν ἀρχὴν
καὶ τὸ τέλος· κγ΄ × ιε΄· φύλλα μδ΄· δίστηλον· γραμμαὶ κε΄·
στρογγύλη γραφή· τῆς θ΄ ἑκατονταετηρίδος· περιέχει ἀποσπάσματά τινα ἑλληνικῶν Εὐαγγελίων τῆς ϛ΄ ἑκατονταετηρίδος ἐν τῷ δεσίμῳ.

Homilies of Evagrius; vellum; imperfect at the beginning and end; 23 × 15; 44 leaves; two columns; 25 lines;
Estrangelo; ninth century; contains fragments of sixth
century Greek Gospels in binding.

61

62

63

64

Εἱρμολόγιον· μεμβράνη· ιε΄ × ι΄· φύλλα ρμη΄· μονόστηλον·
γραμμαὶ ιε΄· νεωτέρας ἐποχῆς.

Hirmologion; vellum; 15 × 10; 148 leaves; one column;
15 lines; late.

65

Εὐαγγέλια κατ᾽ ἀναγνώσεις· ἀκολουθέντα διὰ (ὑπ᾽ ἄλλης
χειρός)·

ܩܪܝܬܐ ܕܩܘܪܒܐ ܕܩܕܝܫܐ ܡܪܝ ܣܘܪܝܣ ܕܩܘܝܬܐ

ܕܚܝܬܐ

μεμβράνη· ιζ´ × ια´· φύλλα πγ´· μονόστηλον· γραμμαὶ κα´.

Lectionary from the Gospels, followed by (in another hand): a Table of Canons for Sundays throughout the year.

Vellum; 17 × 11; 83 leaves; one column; 21 lines.

66

67

Ὁμιλίαι τοῦ Μὰρ Ἐφραίμ· μεμβράνη· ἐλλειπὲς τὴν ἀρχὴν καὶ τὸ τέλος· ιδ´ × ιβ´· φύλλα Ϙγ´· μονόστηλον· γραμμαὶ ιη´· τῆς ἐννάτης ἐκατονταετηρίδος· στρογγύλη γραφή.

Homilies of Mar Ephraim; vellum; imperfect at the beginning and end; 14 × 12; 93 leaves; one column; 18 lines; Estrangelo; ninth century.

68

69

Εἱρμολόγιον· μεμβράνη· ις´ × ι´· φύλλα σιη´· μονόστυλον· γραμμαὶ ιθ´· νεωτέρας ἐποχῆς.

Hirmologion; vellum; 16 × 10; 218 leaves; one column; 19 lines; late.

70

Εἱρμολόγιον· μεμβράνη· λδ´ × κγ´· φύλλα μζ´· δίστηλον· γραμμαὶ κθ´· δωδεκάτης ἐκατονταετηρίδος.

Hirmologion; vellum; 34 × 23; 47 leaves; two columns; 29 lines; twelfth century.

71

Εἱρμολόγιον· μεμβράνη· κζ΄ × ιη΄· φύλλα σπη΄· μονό-
στηλον· γραμμαὶ κγ΄· ἐλλειπὲς τὴν ἀρχὴν ὀκτὼ φύλλων.

Hirmologion; vellum; 27 × 18; 288 leaves; one column;
23 lines; 8 leaves wanting at the beginning.

72

Λειτουργικά· χάρτης· κϛ΄ × ιε΄· φύλλα σξγ΄· μονόστηλον·
γραμμαὶ κα΄· νεωτέρας ἐποχῆς.

Liturgical; paper; 26 × 15; 263 leaves; one column;
21 lines; late.

73

Λειτουργικά· χάρτης· κγ΄ × ιζ΄· φύλλα ρπη΄· μονόστηλον·
γραμμαὶ κε΄· νεωτέρας ἐποχῆς.

Liturgical; paper; 23 × 17; 188 leaves; one column;
25 lines; late.

74

Εὐαγγέλια· χάρτης· ἐλλειπές· κγ΄ × ιδ΄· φύλλα ρμ΄·
μονόστηλον· γραμμαὶ κ΄· νεωτέρας ἐποχῆς· περιέχει τὸ
εὐαγγέλιον Ματθαίου καὶ μέρος τι τοῦ Μάρκου.

Gospels; paper; imperfect; 23 × 14; 140 leaves; one
column; 20 lines; late; contains St Matthew and part of
St Mark.

75

Λειτουργία· μετ᾽ ἀναγνώσεων ἀπὸ τῶν Πράξεων τῶν
Ἀποστόλων· χάρτης· κα΄ × ιβ΄· φύλλα τλη΄· μονόστηλον·
γραμμαὶ ιη΄· νεωτέρας ἐποχῆς.

Liturgy; with lessons from the Acts of the Apostles;
paper; 21 × 12; 338 leaves; one column; 18 lines; late.

76

Εὐαγγέλια κατ᾽ ἀναγνώσεις· χάρτης· κδ΄ × ιδ΄· φύλλα
σκδ΄· μονόστηλον· γραμμαὶ ιζ΄· νεωτέρας ἐποχῆς.

Lectionary ; paper ; 24 × 14 ; 224 leaves ; one column ;
17 lines ; late.

77

Λειτουργικά· χάρτης· κε΄ × ιε΄· φύλλα σοδ΄· μονόστηλον·
γραμμαὶ ιζ΄· νεωτέρας ἐποχῆς.

Liturgical ; paper ; 25 × 15 ; 274 leaves ; one column ;
17 lines ; late.

78

Μηναῖον· χάρτης· κ΄ × ιβ΄· φύλλα τλϛ΄· μονόστηλον·
γραμμαὶ ιη΄· νεωτέρας ἐποχῆς.

Menaion ; paper ; 20 × 12 ; 336 leaves ; one column ;
18 lines ; late.

79

Λειτουργικά· χάρτης· ιη΄ × ιγ΄· φύλλα φμα΄· μονόστηλον·
γραμμαὶ ιε΄.

Liturgical ; paper ; 18 × 13 ; 541 leaves ; one column ;
15 lines.

80

Λειτουργικά· χάρτης· κα΄ × ιβ΄· φύλλα τογ΄· μονόστη-
λον· γραμμαὶ ιη΄· νεωτέρας ἐποχῆς.

Liturgical ; paper ; 21 × 12 ; 373 leaves ; one column ;
18 lines ; late.

81

Πραξαπόστολος· χάρτης· κγ΄ × ιϛ΄· φύλλα ρϟε΄· μονό-
στηλον· γραμμαὶ ιθ΄· νεωτέρας ἐποχῆς.

Acts of the Apostles ; paper ; 23 × 16 ; 195 leaves ; one
column ; 19 lines ; late.

82

Τὸ πρῶτον μέρος περιέχει (α') τὰ Ὑπομνήματα Πειλάτου (οὗ τὸ πρῶτον φύλλον ἐλλείπει)· (β') τὴν Ἀναφορὰν Πειλάτου καὶ ἀλληλογραφίαν μεταξὺ Πειλάτου καὶ Ἡρώδου· (γ') τὴν ἱστορίαν Εὐφημίας· (δ') τὴν ἱστορίαν τῶν τεσσαράκοντα μαρτύρων· (ε') τὰς Πράξεις Ματθαίου καὶ Ἀνδρέου.

Τὸ δεύτερον μέρος (ὑπ' ἄλλης χειρὸς) περιέχει ἐρωτήσεις τε καὶ ἀπαντήσεις.

χάρτης. δωδεκάτης ἑκατονταετηρίδος.

The first part contains (1) the Acts of Pilate (of which the first page is lost), (2) the Anaphora of Pilate, and a correspondence between Pilate and Herod, (3) the story of Euphemia, (4) the story of the forty martyrs, (5) the Acts of Matthew and Andrew.

The second part (in another hand) contains Questions, and Responses.

Paper; twelfth century.

83

Λειτουργικά· χάρτης· κα' × ιβ'· φύλλα συβ'· μονό-στηλον· γραμμαὶ ιε'· νεωτέρας ἐποχῆς.

Liturgical; paper; 21 × 12; 252 leaves; one column; 15 lines; late.

84

Λειτουργικά· χάρτης· κα' × ιβ'· φύλλα τμζ'· μονόστηλον· γραμμαὶ ιε'· νεωτέρας ἐποχῆς.

Liturgical; paper; 21 × 12; 347 leaves; one column; 15 lines; late.

85

Λειτουργικά· χάρτης· κβ' × ιγ'· φύλλα σμ'· μονόστηλον· γραμμαὶ ιζ'.

Liturgical; paper; 22 × 13; 240 leaves; one column; 17 lines.

86

Λειτουργικά· χάρτης· κβ' × ιγ'· φύλλα σοθ'· μονόστηλον· γραμμαὶ ιϛ'· νεωτέρας ἐποχῆς.

Liturgical; paper; 22 × 13; 279 leaves; one column; 16 lines; late.

87

Μηναῖον· χάρτης· κα' × ιδ'· φύλλα τλ'· μονόστηλον· γραμμαὶ ιζ'· νεωτέρας ἐποχῆς.

Menaion; paper; 21 × 14; 330 leaves; one column; 17 lines; late.

88

Μηναῖον· χάρτης· κϛ' × ιϛ'· φύλλα σλβ'· μονόστηλον· γραμμαὶ ιϛ'· νεωτέρας ἐποχῆς.

Menaion; paper; 26 × 16; 232 leaves; one column; 16 lines; late.

89

Λειτουργικὰ μετ' ἀναγνώσεων· χάρτης· κε' × ιε'· μονόστηλον· γραμμαὶ κϛ'· νεωτέρας ἐποχῆς.

Liturgical with lections; paper; 25 × 15; one column; 26 lines; late.

90

Ἀνθολόγιον· χάρτης· ιη' × ια'· φύλλα σξϛ'· μονόστηλον· γραμμαὶ ιζ'· νεωτέρας ἐποχῆς.

Anthologion; paper; 18 × 11; 266 leaves; one column; 17 lines; late.

91

Λειτουργικά· χάρτης· ιη' × ιβ'· φύλλα τιβ'· μονόστηλον· γραμμαὶ ιζ'· νεωτέρας ἐποχῆς.

Liturgical; paper; 18 × 12; 312 leaves; one column; 17 lines: late.

92

Πραξαπόστολος· χάρτης· ιθ' × ιγ'· φύλλα σι'· μονό-
στηλον· γραμμαὶ ιδ'.

Acts of the Apostles; paper; 19 × 13; 210 leaves; one
column; 14 lines.

93

Λειτουργικά· χάρτης· ἐλλειπὲς τὴν ἀρχὴν καὶ τὸ τέλος·
κβ' × ιε'· φύλλα ξδ'· μονόστηλον· γραμμαὶ ιϛ'.

Liturgical; paper; imperfect at the beginning and end;
22 × 15; 64 leaves; one column; 16 lines.

94

Λειτουργία· χάρτης· κα' × ιδ'· μονόστηλον· πολὺ νέον·
τὰ φύλλα συγκεκολλημένα.

Liturgy; paper; 21 × 14; one column; very late; the
leaves much stuck together.

95

Λειτουργικά· χάρτης· κβ' × ιδ'· φύλλα σε'· μονόστηλον·
γραμμαὶ κ'· νεωτέρας ἐποχῆς.

Liturgical; paper; 22 × 14; 205 leaves; one column;
20 lines; late.

96

Εὐχολόγιον· χάρτης· ἐλλειπές· κβ' × ιε'· φύλλα οε'·
μονόστηλον· γραμμαὶ ιη'· νεωτέρας ἐποχῆς.

Prayers; paper; imperfect; 22 × 15; 75 leaves; one
column; 18 lines; late.

97

Λειτουργικά· χάρτης· κα' × ιγ'· φύλλα σξη'· μονόστηλον·
γραμμαὶ κ'· νεωτέρας ἐποχῆς.

Liturgical; paper; 21 × 13; 268 leaves; one column;
20 lines; late.

98

Ψαλτήριον· χάρτης· ιζ' × ια'· φύλλα σιϛ'· μονόστηλον· γραμμαὶ ια'· νεωτέρας ἐποχῆς.

Psalter; paper; 17 × 11; 216 leaves; one column; 11 lines; late.

99

Ψαλτήριον· χάρτης· ιζ' × ια'· φύλλα τιθ'· μονόστηλον· γραμμαὶ ιβ'· νεωτέρας ἐποχῆς.

Psalter; paper; 17 × 11; 319 leaves; one column; 12 lines; late.

100

Πραξαπόστολος· χάρτης· ιη' × ιγ'· φύλλα σμδ'· μονό-στηλον· γραμμαὶ ιε'· νεωτέρας ἐποχῆς.

Acts of the Apostles; paper; 18 × 13; 244 leaves; one column; 15 lines; late.

101

Ψαλτήριον· χάρτης· ιϛ' × ιγ'· φύλλα σ'· μονόστηλον· γραμμαὶ ιδ'· νεωτέρας ἐποχῆς.

Psalter; paper; 16 × 13; 200 leaves; one column; 14 lines; late.

102

Ψαλτήριον· χάρτης· ιε' × ια'· φύλλα ρϟ'· μονόστηλον· γραμμαὶ ιϛ'· νεωτέρας ἐποχῆς.

Psalter; paper; 15 × 11; 190 leaves; one column; 16 lines; late.

103

Ψαλτήριον· ιϛ' × ιβ'· φύλλα σλα'· μονόστηλον· γραμμαὶ ιδ'· νεωτέρας ἐποχῆς.

Psalter; paper; 16 × 12; 231 leaves; one column; 14 lines; late.

104

Λειτουργία· χάρτης· ιθ' × ιγ'· φύλλα σιβ'· μονόστηλον· γραμμαὶ ιδ'· νεωτέρας ἐποχῆς.

Liturgy; paper; 19 × 13; 212 leaves; one column; 14 lines; late.

105

Λειτουργικά· χάρτης· ιη' × ιβ'· φύλλα ρπθ'· μονόστηλον· γραμμαὶ ιβ'· νεωτέρας ἐποχῆς.

Liturgical; paper; 18 × 12; 189 leaves; one column; 12 lines; late.

106

Ὡρολόγιον· χάρτης· ιη' × ιβ'· φύλλα Ϟη'· μονόστηλον· γραμμαὶ ιγ'· νεωτέρας ἐποχῆς.

Horologion; paper; 18 × 12; 98 leaves; one column; 13 lines; late.

107

Λειτουργικά· χάρτης· κα' × ιδ'· φύλλα σνδ'· μονόστηλον· γραμμαὶ ιη'· νεωτέρας ἐποχῆς.

Liturgical; paper; 21 × 14; 254 leaves; one column; 18 lines; late.

108

109

Εὐχολόγιον· χάρτης· ιθ' × ιγ'· φύλλα σκζ'· μονόστηλον· γραμμαὶ ιδ'· νεωτέρας ἐποχῆς.

Prayers; paper; 19 × 13; 227 leaves; one column; 14 lines; late.

110

Μηναῖον· χάρτης· κα′ × ιδ′ φύλλα σμθ′· μονόστηλον· γραμμαὶ ιϛ′· νεωτέρας ἐποχῆς.

Menaion; paper; 21 × 14; 249 leaves; one column; 16 lines; late.

111

Ἀνθολόγιον (ܐܠܐ ܝܙܘܐ ܐܢܐܟܐ ܐܚܘܠܐܘܐ)· ἀκολουθία τῆς τοῦ Μὰρ Ἡλίου ἑορτῆς· χάρτης· ιζ′ × ια′· φύλλα τοϛ′· μονόστηλον· γραμμαὶ ιε′· νεωτέρας ἐποχῆς.

Anthologion; office for the feast of Mar Elias; paper; 17 × 11; 376 leaves; one column; 15 lines; late.

112

Ψαλτήριον· χάρτης· ιε′ × ια′· φύλλα σξβ′· μονόστηλον· γραμμαὶ ιγ′· νεωτέρας ἐποχῆς.

Psalter; paper; 15 × 11; 262 leaves; one column; 13 lines; late.

113

Εὐχολόγιον· χάρτης· ἐλλειπές· ιζ′ × ιγ′· φύλλα μζ′· μονόστηλον· γραμμαὶ ιδ′· νεωτέρας ἐποχῆς.

Prayers; paper; imperfect; 17 × 13; 47 leaves; one column; 14 lines; late.

114

Εὐχολόγιον· χάρτης· ιζ′ × ιγ′· φύλλα ϟ′· μονόστηλον· γραμμαὶ ιγ′.

Prayers; paper; 17 × 13; 90 leaves; one. column; 13 lines.

115

Εὐχολόγιον· χάρτης· ιϛ′ × ιβ′· φύλλα ξϛ′· μονόστηλον· γραμμαὶ ιδ′· νεωτέρας ἐποχῆς.

Prayers; paper; 16 × 12; 66 leaves; one column; 14 lines; late.

116

Ὡρολόγιον· χάρτης· ιϛ′ × ια′· φύλλα ρπδ′· μονόστηλον· γραμμαὶ ιγ′· νεωτέρας ἐποχῆς.

Horologion; paper; 16 × 11; 184 leaves; one column; 13 lines; late.

117

Εὐχολόγιον· χάρτης· ιη′ × ιδ′· φύλλα πα′· μονόστηλον· γραμμαὶ ιδ′· νεωτέρας ἐποχῆς.

Prayers; paper; 18 × 14; 81 leaves; one column; 14 lines; late.

118

Στιχεράριον· χάρτης· ιζ′ × ιβ′· φύλλα τκ′· μονόστηλον· γραμμαὶ κϛ′· νεωτέρας ἐποχῆς.

Sticherarion; paper; 17 × 12; 320 leaves; one column; 26 lines; late.

119

Λειτουργικά· χάρτης· ιζ′ × ιβ′· φύλλα σμβ′· μονόστηλον· γραμμαὶ ιδ′· νεωτέρας ἐποχῆς.

Liturgical; paper; 17 × 12; 242 leaves; one column; late.

120

Ἀναγνώσεις καὶ λειτουργικά· χάρτης· ιζ′ × ιβ′· φύλλα συθ′· μονόστηλον· γραμμαὶ ιζ′· νεωτέρας ἐποχῆς.

Lections and liturgical matter; paper; 17 × 12; 259 leaves; one column; 17 lines; late.

121

Ψαλτήριον· χάρτης· πολὺ διεφθαρμένον διὰ τῆς ὑγρότη-
τος· ιζ′ × ιβ′· φύλλα σκζ· μονόστηλον· γραμμαὶ ιε′· νεωτέρας
ἐποχῆς.

Psalter; paper; much damaged by wet; 17 × 12; 227
leaves; one column; 15 lines; late.

122

Εἱρμολόγιον· χάρτης· ιζ′ × ιβ′· φύλλα ρι′· μονόστηλον·
γραμμαὶ ιζ′· νεωτέρας ἐποχῆς.

Hirmologion; paper; 17 × 12; 110 leaves; one column;
17 lines; late.

123

Εὐχολόγιον ܟܬܒ̈ܐ ܕܨܠܘܬܐ· χάρτης· ιη′ × ιδ′·
φύλλα τν′· μονόστηλον· γραμμαὶ ιδ′· νεωτέρας ἐποχῆς.

Prayers; paper; 18 × 14; 350 leaves; one column; 14
lines; late.

124

Ψαλτήριον· χάρτης· ιϛ′ × ια′· φύλλα τμ′· μονόστηλον·
γραμμαὶ ιγ′· νεωτέρας ἐποχῆς.

Psalter; paper; 16 × 11; 340 leaves; one column; 13
lines; late.

125

Ψαλτήριον· χάρτης· ιϛ′ × ιγ′· φύλλα σν′· μονόστηλον·
γραμμαὶ ια′· νεωτέρας ἐποχῆς.

Psalter; paper; 16 × 13; 250 leaves; one column; 11
lines; late.

126

'Ανθολόγιον· χάρτης· ιζ' × ιγ'· φύλλα σλβ'· μονόστηλον· γραμμαὶ ιβ'· νεωτέρας ἐποχῆς.

Anthologion; paper; 17 × 13; 232 leaves; one column; 12 lines; late.

127

Λειτουργικά· χάρτης· ιη' × ιβ'· φύλλα ρ9ς'· μονόστηλον· γραμμαὶ ιδ'· νεωτέρας ἐποχῆς.

Liturgical; paper; 18 × 12; 196 leaves; one column; 14 lines; late.

128

Ψαλτήριον· χάρτης· ιζ' × ιγ'· φύλλα σξδ'· μονόστηλον· γραμμαὶ ιε'· νεωτέρας ἐποχῆς.

Psalter; paper; 17 × 13; 264 leaves; one column; 15 lines; late.

129

Λειτουργικά· Τυπικὸν κατὰ τὸ ἔθος τῆς Ἰερουσαλήμ· χάρτης· ιζ' × ιβ'· φύλλα ρμ'· μονόστηλον· γραμμαὶ ιη'· νεωτέρας ἐποχῆς· περιέχει φύλλα τινὰ ἀραβικά.

Liturgical; Typicon according to the Jerusalem use; paper; 17 × 12; 140 leaves; one column; 18 lines; late; contains some Arabic leaves.

130

'Ωρολόγιον· χάρτης· ιε' × ιβ'· φύλλα σνα'· μονόστηλον· γραμμαὶ ιε'· νεωτέρας ἐποχῆς.

Horologion; paper; 15 × 12; 251 leaves; one column; 15 lines; late.

131

Λειτουργικά· χάρτης· ἐλλειπὲς τὴν ἀρχήν· ιϛ' × ια'· φύλλα σπη'· μονόστηλον· γραμμαὶ ιϛ'· νεωτέρας ἐποχῆς.

Liturgical; paper; imperfect at the beginning; 16 × 11; 288 leaves; one column; 16 lines; late.

132

ܟܬܒܐ ܕܩܠܝܬܐ ܕܕܝܪܐ

Λειτουργικά· ἀναγνώσεις κ.τ.λ.· χάρτης· ιθ' × ιγ'· φύλλα σιε'· μονόστηλον· γραμμαὶ ιε'· νεωτέρας ἐποχῆς.

Liturgical; lections, etc.; paper; 19 × 13; 215 leaves; one column; 15 lines; late.

133

Στιχεράριον· χάρτης· ἐλλειπὲς τὴν ἀρχὴν καὶ τὸ τέλος· ιζ' × ιη'· φύλλα ση'· μονόστηλον· γραμμαὶ ιβ'· νεωτέρας ἐποχῆς.

Sticherarion; paper; imperfect at the beginning and end; 17 × 18; 208 leaves; one column; 12 lines; late.

134

Εὐαγγέλια· χάρτης· ἐλλειπὲς τὴν ἀρχὴν καὶ τὸ τέλος· κα' × ιγ'· φύλλα Ϙβ'· μονόστηλον· γραμμαὶ ιθ'· νεωτέρας ἐποχῆς.

Gospels; paper; imperfect at the beginning and end; 21 × 13; 92 leaves; one column; 19 lines; late.

135

Εὐαγγέλια· χάρτης· ιζ' × ιγ'· φύλλα ρπ' μονόστηλον· γραμμαὶ κα'· νεωτέρας ἐποχῆς.

Gospels; paper; 17 × 13; 180 leaves; one column; 21 lines; late.

136

Τυπικόν· χάρτης· ιζ' × ιγ'· φύλλα σμθ'· μονόστηλον· γραμμαὶ ιε'· νεωτέρας ἐποχῆς.

Typicon ; paper ; 17 × 13 ; 249 leaves ; one column ; 15 lines ; late.

137

Λειτουργικά· χάρτης· ιθ' × ιβ'· φύλλα σβ'· μονόστηλον· γραμμαὶ ιζ'· νεωτέρας ἐποχῆς.

Liturgical ; paper ; 19 × 12 ; 202 leaves ; one column ; 17 lines ; late.

138

Λειτουργικά· ὧν ἡ ἀρχή ἐστιν ὁ κανὼν διὰ τὰ χριστού-γεννα· χάρτης· ιε' × ια'· φύλλα σπη'· μονόστηλον· γραμμαὶ ιγ'.

Liturgical ; beginning with the order for Christmas day ; paper ; 15 × 11 ; 288 leaves ; one column ; 13 lines.

139

Ψαλτήριον· χάρτης· ιε' × ια'· φύλλα σοθ'· μονόστηλον· γραμμαὶ ι'· νεωτέρας ἐποχῆς.

Psalter ; paper ; 15 × 11 ; 279 leaves ; one column ; 10 lines ; late.

140

Κανὼν τοῦ Βαπτισμοῦ· χάρτης· ις' × ια'· φύλλα σπγ'· μονόστηλον· γραμμαὶ ια'· νεωτέρας ἐποχῆς.

Order of Baptism, etc.; paper ; 16 × 11 ; 283 leaves ; one column ; 11 lines ; late.

141

Εἱρμολόγιον· χάρτης· ιε' × ι'· φύλλα σ'· μονόστηλον· γραμμαὶ ιγ'· νεωτέρας ἐποχῆς.

Hirmologion ; paper ; 15 × 10 ; 200 leaves ; one column ; 13 lines ; late.

142

Ὡρολόγιον· χάρτης· ις΄ × ιβ΄· φύλλα ρο΄· μονόστηλον· γραμμαὶ ια΄· νεωτέρας ἐποχῆς.

Horologion ; paper ; 16 × 12 ; 170 leaves ; one column ; 11 lines ; late.

143

Ψαλτήριον· χάρτης· ις΄ × ιβ΄· φύλλα σοε΄· μονόστηλον· γραμμαὶ ιβ΄· νεωτέρας ἐποχῆς.

Psalter ; paper ; 16 × 12 ; 275 leaves ; one column ; 12 lines ; late.

144

145

Εὐαγγέλιον· χάρτης· ιζ΄ × ια΄· φύλλα ρϞη΄· μονόστηλον· γραμμαὶ κ΄· νεωτέρας ἐποχῆς.

Gospel ; paper ; 17 × 11 ; 198 leaves ; one column ; 20 lines ; late.

146

Ὕμνοι· χάρτης· ιζ΄ × ια΄· φύλλα ρε΄· μονόστηλον· γραμμαὶ ιβ΄· νεωτέρας ἐποχῆς.

Hymns ; paper ; 17 × 11 ; 105 leaves ; one column ; 12 lines ; late.

147

Λειτουργικά· χάρτης· ιη΄ × ιγ΄· φύλλα πη΄· μονόστηλον· γραμμαὶ ια΄· νεωτέρας ἐποχῆς.

Liturgical ; paper ; 18 × 13 ; 88 leaves ; one column ; 11 lines ; late.

148

Στιχεράριον· χάρτης· ιζ′ × ιβ′· φύλλα ρπβ′· μονόστη-
λον· γραμμαὶ ιζ′· νεωτέρας ἐποχῆς.

Sticherarion ; paper; 17 × 12; 182 leaves; one column;
17 lines ; late.

149

Ψαλτήριον· χάρτης· ιϛ′ × ια′· φύλλα σλγ′· μονόστηλον·
γραμμαὶ ιδ′· νεωτέρας ἐποχῆς.

Psalter; paper; 16 × 11; 233 leaves; one column; 14
lines ; late.

150

Ὡρολόγιον· χάρτης· ιε′ × ιγ′· φύλλα ρκ′· μονόστηλον·
γραμμαὶ ιϛ′· νεωτέρας ἐποχῆς.

Horologion ; paper ; 15 × 13; 120 leaves; one column;
16 lines ; late.

151

Ὡρολόγιον· χάρτης· ιϛ′ × ιγ′· φύλλα ρκβ′· μονόστηλον·
γραμμαὶ ι′· νεωτέρας ἐποχῆς.

Horologion ; paper ; 16 × 13; 122 leaves; one column;
10 lines ; late.

152

Εὐχολόγιον· χάρτης· ιδ′ × ι′· φύλλα σογ′· μονόστηλον·
γραμμαὶ ι′· νεωτέρας ἐποχῆς.

Prayers ; paper ; 14 × 10; 273 leaves; one column; 10
lines ; late.

153

Ὡρολόγιον· χάρτης· ιδ′ × θ′· φύλλα σϟ′· μονόστηλον·
γραμμαὶ ιγ′· νεωτέρας ἐποχῆς.

Horologion ; paper ; 14 × 9; 290 leaves; one column;
13 lines ; late.

154

Εἱρμολόγιον· χάρτης· ιγ΄ × ι΄· φύλλα ρϟδ΄· μονόστηλον· γραμμαὶ ι΄· νεωτέρας ἐποχῆς.

Hirmologion; paper; 13 × 10; 194 leaves; one column; 10 lines; late.

155

Ψαλτήριον· χάρτης· ιδ΄ × ι΄· φύλλα σμϛ΄· μονόστηλον· γραμμαὶ ιε΄· νεωτέρας ἐποχῆς.

Psalter; paper; 14 × 10; 246 leaves; one column; 15 lines; late.

156

"Υμνοι· χάρτης· ιθ΄ × ι΄· φύλλα τη΄· μονόστηλον· γραμμαὶ ι΄· νεωτέρας ἐποχῆς.

Hymns; paper; 19 × 10; 308 leaves; one column; 10 lines; late.

157

Ψαλτήριον· χάρτης· ιγ΄ × ι΄· φύλλα σξζ΄· μονόστηλον· γραμμαὶ ιγ΄· νεωτέρας ἐποχῆς.

Psalter; paper; 13 × 10; 267 leaves; one column; 13 lines; late.

158

Ὡρολόγιον· χάρτης· ιε΄ × ι΄· φύλλα ροϛ΄· μονόστηλον· γραμμαὶ ιβ΄· νεωτέρας ἐποχῆς.

Horologion; paper; 15 × 10; 176 leaves; one column; 12 lines; late.

159

Εὐαγγέλια· χάρτης· ιδ΄ × θ΄· φύλλα ρκδ΄· μονόστηλον· γραμμαὶ ιβ΄· νεωτέρας ἐποχῆς.

Gospels; paper; 14 × 9; 124 leaves; one column; 12 lines; late.

160

161

'Αναγνώσεις· χάρτης· ἐλλειπὲς τὴν ἀρχήν· ιϛ' × ιβ'·
φύλλα λθ'· μονόστηλον· γραμμαὶ ιβ'· νεωτέρας ἐποχῆς.

Lectionary; paper; imperfect at the beginning ; 16×12 ;
39 leaves ; one column ; 12 lines ; late.

162

Ψαλτήριον· χάρτης· ἐλλειπὲς τὴν ἀρχήν· ιζ' × ιγ'· φύλλα
ρνη'· μονόστηλον· γραμμαὶ ιϛ'· νεωτέρας ἐποχῆς.

Psalter ; paper ; imperfect at the beginning ; 17 × 13 ;
158 leaves ; one column ; 16 lines ; late.

163

Πεντηκοστάριον· χάρτης· ἐλλειπές· ιϛ' × ιβ'· φύλλα ο'·
μονόστηλον· γραμμαὶ ιβ'· νεωτέρας ἐποχῆς.

Pentecostarion ; paper ; imperfect ; 16 × 12 ; 70 leaves ;
one column ; 12 lines ; late.

164

Τροπάριον· χάρτης· ιϛ' × ιβ'· φύλλα Ϟθ'· μονόστηλον·
γραμμαὶ ιβ'· νεωτέρας ἐποχῆς.

Troparion ; paper ; 16 × 12 ; 99 leaves ; one column ; 12
lines ; late.

165

Ψαλτήριον· χάρτης· ιδ' × ι'· φύλλα σπβ'· μονόστηλον·
γραμμαὶ ιγ'· νεωτέρας ἐποχῆς.

Psalter ; paper ; 14 × 10 ; 282 leaves ; one column ; 13
lines ; late.

166

Ὡρολόγιον· χάρτης· ιγ΄ × ι΄· φύλλα ρλθ΄· μονόστηλον· γραμμαὶ ι΄· νεωτέρας ἐποχῆς.

Horologion ; paper ; 13 × 10 ; 139 leaves ; one column ; 10 lines ; late.

167

Λειτουργικά· ἐλλειπὲς τὴν ἀρχήν· χάρτης· ιδ΄ × ια΄· φύλλα ρε΄· μονόστηλον· γραμμαὶ ιϛ΄.

Liturgical; paper; imperfect at the beginning; 14 × 11 ; 105 leaves ; one column ; 16 lines.

168

Λειτουργίαι· χάρτης· ιδ΄ × ι΄· μονόστηλον· γραμμαὶ ιϛ΄· νεωτέρας ἐποχῆς.

Liturgies ; paper ; 14 × 10 ; one column ; 16 lines ; late.

169

Ὡρολόγιον· χάρτης· ιγ΄ × ι΄· φύλλα ρϟ΄· μονόστηλον· γραμμαὶ ιβ΄· νεωτέρας ἐποχῆς.

Horologion ; paper ; 13 × 10 ; 190 leaves ; one column ; 12 lines ; late.

170

Ψαλτήριον· χάρτης· ιγ΄ × θ΄· φύλλα σν΄· μονόστηλον· γραμμαὶ ιε΄.

Psalter ; paper ; 13 × 9 ; 250 leaves ; one column ; 15 lines.

171

Εὐχολόγιον· χάρτης· ιδ΄ × θ΄· φύλλα ρϟζ΄· μονόστηλον· γραμμαὶ ιδ΄.

Prayers ; paper ; 14 × 9 ; 197 leaves ; one column ; 14 lines.

172

Εὐαγγέλια μετὰ σημειώσεων ἁρμονιστικῶν· χάρτης·
ιγ΄ × θ΄· φύλλα σ΄· μονόστηλον· γραμμαὶ κβ΄· νεωτέρας
ἐποχῆς.

Gospels with harmony references; paper; 13 × 9; 200
leaves; one column; 22 lines; late.

173

ܪ̈ܒܘܬ ܟܬܒܐ· περιέχει εὐχάς· π.χ. εὐχὴν ὑπὲρ
τὸν φάγοντα ῥυπαρόν τι· χάρτης· ιγ΄ × θ΄· φύλλα ρξη΄·
μονόστηλον· γραμμαὶ ιγ΄· νεωτέρας ἐποχῆς.

Contains prayers, for example, a prayer for a man who
has eaten something unclean; paper; 13 × 9; 168 leaves;
one column; 13 lines; late.

174

Εὐχολόγιον· χάρτης· ιγ΄ × ι΄· φύλλα ρϟβ΄· μονόστηλον·
γραμμαὶ ιβ΄.

Prayers; paper; 13 × 10; 192 leaves; one column; 12
lines.

175

Λειτουργικά· χάρτης· ιδ΄ × ια΄· φύλλα ρπγ΄· μονόστηλον·
γραμμαὶ ιγ΄.

Liturgical; paper; 14 × 11; 183 leaves; one column;
13 lines.

176

Ψαλτήριον· χάρτης· ιβ΄ × η΄· φύλλα σμε΄· μονόστηλον·
γραμμαὶ ιβ΄.

Psalter; paper; 12 × 8; 245 leaves; one column; 12
lines.

177

Εὐχολόγιον· χάρτης· ιγ΄ × η΄· φύλλα σθ΄· μονόστηλον· γραμμαὶ ιδ΄· νεωτέρας ἐποχῆς.

Ἄρχει ...ܪܚܐܠܠܐܠ ܪܝܐܝܣ

Prayers; paper; 13 × 8; 209 leaves; one column; 14 lines; late.

178

Λειτουργικά· Εὐχολόγιον· χάρτης· ια΄ × ε΄· φύλλα σε΄· μονόστηλον· γραμμαὶ ια΄· νεωτέρας ἐποχῆς.

Liturgical; prayers; paper; 11 × 5; 205 leaves; one column; 11 lines; late.

179

Ὡρολόγιον· χάρτης· ι΄ × ϛ΄· φύλλα ρο΄· μονόστηλον· γραμμαὶ ιβ΄· νεωτέρας ἐποχῆς.

Horologion; paper; 10 × 6; 170 leaves; one column; 12 lines; late.

180

Λειτουργικά· χάρτης· ι΄ × ζ΄· φύλλα σδ΄· μονόστηλον· γραμμαὶ ι΄· νεωτέρας ἐποχῆς.

Liturgical; paper; 10 × 7; 204 leaves; one column; 10 lines; late.

181

Εὐαγγέλια κατ᾽ ἀναγνώσεις· χάρτης· κ΄ × ιγ΄· φύλλα οβ΄· μονόστηλον· γραμμαὶ ιζ΄· νεωτέρας ἐποχῆς.

Lectionary; paper; 20 × 13; 72 leaves; one column; 17 lines; late.

182

Λειτουργικά· χάρτης· ἐλλειπὲς τὴν ἀρχὴν ἐννέα φύλλων· κε΄ × ιζ΄· φύλλα ρμ΄· μονόστηλον· γραμμαὶ ιζ΄· νεωτέρας ἐποχῆς.

Liturgical ; paper ; nine pages lost at the beginning ; 25 × 17 ; 140 leaves ; one column ; 17 lines ; late.

183

Λειτουργικά· χάρτης· ἐλλειπὲς τὴν ἀρχὴν ρπδ΄ φύλλων· κζ΄ × ιθ΄· φύλλα σι΄· μονόστηλον· γραμμαὶ κ΄· νεωτέρας ἐποχῆς.

Liturgical ; paper ; 184 leaves lost at the beginning ; 27 × 19 ; 210 leaves ; one column ; 20 lines ; late.

184

Λειτουργικά· χάρτης· κϛ΄ × ιϛ΄· φύλλα σιθ΄· μονόστηλον· γραμμαὶ ιδ΄· νεωτέρας ἐποχῆς.

Liturgical ; paper ; 26 × 16 ; 219 leaves ; one column ; 14 lines ; late.

185

Λειτουργικά· χάρτης· κδ΄ × ιε΄· φύλλα σκε΄· μονόστηλον· γραμμαὶ ιη΄· νεωτέρας ἐποχῆς.

Liturgical ; paper ; 24 × 15 ; 225 leaves ; one column ; 18 lines ; late.

186

Λειτουργικά· χάρτης· ἐλλειπὲς τὴν ἀρχήν· κε΄ × ιϛ΄· φύλλα σιβ΄· μονόστηλον· γραμμαὶ κ΄· νεωτέρας ἐποχῆς.

Liturgical ; paper ; imperfect at the beginning ; 25 × 16 ; 212 pages ; one column ; 20 lines ; late.

187

Παρακλητική· χάρτης· κε΄ × ιε΄· φύλλα ρϛ΄· μονόστηλον·
γραμμαὶ ιθ΄· ἐλλειπὲς τὴν ἀρχὴν ἐξ φύλλων· νεωτέρας
ἐποχῆς.

Ἄρχει ܝܡܐ.ܢ ܟܢܝܘܟ ܟܝܩܝܩ ܒܩܕ

Paracletic; paper; 25 × 15; 106 leaves; one column;
19 lines; six leaves wanting at the beginning; late.

188

Λειτουργία· χάρτης· ἐλλειπὲς τὴν ἀρχήν· κε΄ × ιε΄· φύλλα
ρϙδ΄· μονόστηλον· γραμμαὶ κγ΄· νεωτέρας ἐποχῆς.

Liturgy; paper; imperfect at the beginning; 25 × 15;
194 leaves; one column; 23 lines; late.

189

Συναξάριον· ἢ Εὐαγγέλια κατ᾿ ἀναγνώσεις κατὰ τοὺς
Ἕλληνας· χάρτης· ἐλλειπὲς τὸ τέλος· κε΄ × ιζ΄· φύλλα ροθ΄·
δίστηλον· γραμμαὶ ιζ΄· νεωτέρας ἐποχῆς.

Synaxarion, or Lectionary, according to the order of
the Greeks; paper; imperfect at the end; 25 × 17; 179
leaves; two columns; 17 lines; late.

190

Ὑμνολόγιον· χάρτης· ἐλλειπὲς τὴν ἀρχὴν ὀκτὼ φύλλων·
κα΄ × ιδ΄· φύλλα σμθ΄· μονόστηλον· γραμμαὶ ιε΄· νεωτέρας
ἐποχῆς.

Hymnologion; paper; eight leaves lost at the beginning;
21 × 14; 249 leaves; one column; 15 lines; late.

191

Λειτουργικά· χάρτης· ἐλλειπὲς τὴν ἀρχὴν καὶ τὸ τέλος·
κε΄ × ιζ΄· φύλλα σμβ΄· μονόστηλον· γραμμαὶ ιθ΄.

Liturgical; paper; imperfect at beginning and end;
25 × 17; 242 leaves; one column; 19 lines.

192

Τυπικόν· χάρτης· κϛ' × ιη'· φύλλα σε'· μονόστηλον· γραμμαὶ κ'.

Typicon; paper; 26 × 18; 205 leaves; one column; 20 lines.

193

Λειτουργικά· χάρτης· ἐλλειπὲς τὴν ἀρχήν· κβ' × ιε'· φύλλα ρλϛ'· μονόστηλον· γραμμαὶ ιε'· νεωτέρας ἐποχῆς.

Liturgical; paper; imperfect at the beginning; 22 × 15; 136 leaves; one column; 15 lines; late.

194

Λειτουργικά· ἐλλειπὲς τὴν ἀρχὴν καὶ τὸ τέλος· κβ' × ιϛ'· φύλλα ρξα'· δίστηλον· γραμμαὶ κ'· νεωτέρας ἐποχῆς.

Liturgical; imperfect at beginning and end; 22 × 16; 161 leaves; two columns; 20 lines; late.

195

Λειτουργικά· χάρτης, ἐλλειπὲς τὴν ἀρχήν· κα' × ιγ'· φύλλα τι'· μονόστηλον· γραμμαὶ ιζ'· νεωτέρας ἐποχῆς.

Liturgical; paper; imperfect at the beginning; 21 × 13; 310 leaves; one column; 17 lines; late.

196

Λειτουργικά· χάρτης· ἐλλειπὲς τὴν ἀρχήν· κα' × ιη'· φύλλα σιδ'· μονόστηλον· γραμμαὶ ιε'· νεωτέρας ἐποχῆς.

Liturgical; paper; imperfect at the beginning; 21 × 18; 214 leaves; one column; 15 lines; late.

197

Τροπάριον· χάρτης· ἐλλειπὲς τὴν ἀρχὴν ἑπτὰ φύλλων·
κϛ΄ × ιη΄· φύλλα σπε΄· δίστηλον· γραμμαὶ κβ΄· χωρὶς δεσίμου.

Troparion; paper; seven leaves wanting at the beginning; 26 × 18; 285 leaves; two columns; 22 lines; no
binding.

198

Λειτουργικά· χάρτης· ἐλλειπὲς τὴν ἀρχὴν καὶ τὸ τέλος·
κε΄ × ιζ΄· φύλλα σε΄· μονόστηλον· γραμμαὶ ιη΄.

Liturgical; paper; imperfect at beginning and end;
25 × 17; 205 leaves; one column; 18 lines.

199

Προφητολόγιον· χάρτης· κ΄ × ιβ΄· φύλλα σκ΄· δίστηλον·
γραμμαὶ ιζ΄· τοῦ ἔτους ͵ασξ΄.

Prophetologion; paper; 20 × 12; 220 leaves; two
columns; 17 lines; date 1260.

200

Εὐαγγέλια κατ᾽ ἀναγνώσεις· χάρτης· ἐλλειπὲς τὴν ἀρχήν·
ιδ΄ × ι΄· φύλλα υιζ΄· μονόστηλον· γραμμαὶ ιγ΄.

Lectionary; paper; imperfect at the beginning; 14 × 10;
417 leaves; one column; 13 lines.

201

Ψαλτήριον· χάρτης· ιγ΄ × ι΄· φύλλα σκδ΄· μονόστηλον·
γραμμαὶ ιγ΄.

Psalter; paper; 13 × 10; 224 leaves; one column; 13
lines.

202

Λειτουργικά· χάρτης· ἐλλειπὲς τὴν ἀρχήν· κζ΄×ιζ΄· φύλλα
τοε΄· μονόστηλον· γραμμαὶ κδ΄· νεωτέρας ἐποχῆς.

Liturgical; paper; imperfect at the beginning; 27 × 17;
375 pages; one column; 24 lines; late.

203

Λειτουργικά· χάρτης· κϛ΄ × ιζ΄· φύλλα τϟη΄· μονόστηλον·
γραμμαὶ κα΄. Ἄρχει ... ܒܘܬܗ ܡܩܠܐ ܕܟ

Liturgical; paper; 26 × 17; 398 leaves; one column;
21 lines.

204

Μηναῖον κατὰ τοὺς Μαρωνίτας· χάρτης· κε΄ × ιϛ΄· φύλλα
σμ΄· μονόστηλον· γραμμαὶ ιθ΄.

Menæon according to the Maronite usage; paper;
25 × 16; 240 leaves; one column; 19 lines.

205

Εὐαγγέλια· χάρτης· κε΄ × ιζ΄· φύλλα τλ΄· δίστηλον·
γραμμαὶ κ΄· ἐλλειπὲς τὴν ἀρχὴν ὀκτὼ φύλλων.

Gospels; paper; 25 × 17; 330 leaves; two columns;
20 lines; eight leaves wanting at the beginning.

206

Λειτουργικά· χάρτης· ἐλλειπὲς τὴν ἀρχὴν καὶ τὸ τέλος·
χωρὶς δεσίμου· κε΄ × ιϛ΄· φύλλα σδ΄· μονόστηλον· γραμμαὶ
ιη΄.

Liturgical; paper; imperfect at beginning and end;
binding lost; 25 × 16; 204 leaves; one column; 18 lines.

207

Τριῴδιον· χάρτης· κϛ' × ιη'· φύλλα τη'· μονόστηλον· γραμμαὶ ιζ'· νεωτέρας ἐποχῆς.

Triodion ; paper ; 26 × 18 ; 308 leaves ; one column ; 17 lines ; late.

208

Παρακλητική· χάρτης· κϛ' × ιζ'· φύλλα σοζ'· μονόστη-λον· γραμμαὶ κ'· νεωτέρας ἐποχῆς· περιέχει ἐν τῷ δεσίμῳ φύλλα τινὰ ὁμιλιῶν τοῦ ܩ‎ܘܪܩ‎ܘܪ‎ ܝ‎ܣ‎.

Parakletike ; paper ; 26 × 17 ; 277 leaves ; one column ; 20 lines ; late. In the cover are some leaves of homilies.

209

Παρακλητική· χάρτης· κε' × ιζ'· φύλλα ρϙ'· μονόστη-λον· γραμμαὶ ιη'· νεωτέρας ἐποχῆς. Ἄρχει ...ܪ‎ܝܪܟ‎ ܦ‎ ܩ‎ ܕ‎ ܗ‎ ܡ‎ ܘ‎ ܣ‎.

Parakletike ; paper ; 25 × 17 ; 190 leaves ; one column ; 18 lines ; late.

210

Παρακλητική· χάρτης· κζ' × ιθ'· φύλλα σβ'· μονόστη-λον· γραμμαὶ ιθ'· νεωτέρας ἐποχῆς.

Parakletike ; paper ; 27 × 19 ; 202 leaves ; one column ; 19 lines ; late.

211

Λειτουργικά· χάρτης· ἐλλειπὲς τὴν ἀρχὴν καὶ τὸ τέλος· κζ' × ιε'· φύλλα πγ'· μονόστηλον· γραμμαὶ κ'· νεωτέρας ἐποχῆς.

Liturgical ; paper ; imperfect at the beginning and end ; 27 × 15 ; 83 leaves ; one column ; 20 lines ; late.

212

Μηναῖον· χάρτης· κε′ × ιϛ′· φύλλα σα′· μονόστηλον· γραμμαὶ κα′· νεωτέρας ἐποχῆς· περιέχει φύλλα ἀρχαῖά τινα ἐν τῷ δεσίμῳ μεθ᾽ ὁμιλίας περὶ τῆς κλήσεως Μωυσέως καὶ τῆς κτίσεως τοῦ κόσμου.

Menæon; paper; 25 × 16; 201 leaves; one column; 21 lines; late. In the cover are some early leaves with a Homily about the Calling of Moses and the Creation.

213

Προφητολόγιον· χάρτης· κε′ × ιζ′· φύλλα ροζ′· μονόστη-λον· γραμμαὶ κ′· νεωτέρας ἐποχῆς.

Prophetologion; paper; 25 × 17; 177 leaves; one column; 20 lines; late.

214

Ἀπόστολος· χάρτης· κε′ × ιη′· φύλλα ρλδ′· δίστηλον· γραμμαὶ ιθ′.

Lectionary from the Acts and Epistles; paper; 25 × 18; 134 leaves; two columns; 19 lines.

215

Ἀπόστολος· χάρτης· κγ′ × ιδ′· φύλλα σβ′· δίστηλον· γραμμαὶ κ′.

Lectionary from the Acts and Epistles; paper; 23 × 14; 202 leaves; two columns; 20 lines.

216

Ἀπόστολος· χάρτης· κγ′ × ιθ′· φύλλα ρξθ′· μονόστηλον· γραμμαὶ ιζ′· περιέχει ἐν τῷ δεσίμῳ ἀρχαῖα στρόγγυλα φύλλα τινὰ ἀπὸ τοῦ Εὐαγγελίου Ἰωάννου. (Πεσσίτο.)

Lectionary from the Acts and Epistles; paper; 23 × 19; 169 leaves; one column; 17 lines. It contains in the cover some early Estrangelo leaves from the Gospel of John. (Peshito.)

217

Εὐαγγέλια· χάρτης· ἐλλειπὲς τὴν ἀρχήν· κβ' × ιε'· φύλλα ρ¶ς'· μονόστηλον· γραμμαὶ ιζ'· νεωτέρας ἐποχῆς.

Gospels; paper; imperfect at the beginning; 22 × 15; 196 leaves; one column; 17 lines; late.

218

᾿Απόστολος· χάρτης· κβ' × ιε'· φύλλα ρνα'· δίστηλον· γραμμαὶ ιθ'· νεωτέρας ἐποχῆς.

Lectionary from Acts and Epistles; paper; 22 × 15; 151 leaves; two columns; 19 lines; late.

219

Εὐαγγέλια· χάρτης· ιζ' × ιγ'· φύλλα σξβ'· μονόστηλον· γραμμαὶ ιζ'· νεωτέρας ἐποχῆς.

Gospels; paper; 17 × 13; 262 leaves; one column; 17 lines; late.

220

Λειτουργικά· χάρτης· ἐλλειπὲς τὴν ἀρχὴν καὶ τὸ τέλος· κα' × ιδ'· φύλλα σμε'· μονόστηλον· γραμμαὶ ιη'· νεωτέρας ἐποχῆς.

Liturgical; paper; imperfect at beginning and end; 21 × 14; 245 leaves; one column; 18 lines; late.

221

Στιχηράριον· χάρτης· ἐλλειπὲς τὴν ἀρχήν· ις' × ιβ'· φύλλα σπς'· μονόστηλον· γραμμαὶ ιγ'.

Sticherarion; paper; imperfect at the beginning; 16 × 12; 286 leaves; one column; 13 lines.

222

Εὐαγγέλια κατ᾿ ἀναγνώσεις· χάρτης· ιθ' × ιβ'· φύλλα ρπ'· μονόστηλον· γραμμαὶ ιε'.

Lectionary; paper; 19 × 12; 180 leaves; one column; 15 lines.

223

Συναξάριον· χάρτης· ἐλλειπὲς τὴν ἀρχήν· ιη΄ × ιγ΄·
φύλλα σιε΄· μονόστηλον· γραμμαὶ ιδ΄· νεωτέρας ἐποχῆς.

Synaxarion; paper; imperfect at the beginning; 18 × 13,
215 leaves; one column; 14 lines; late.

224

Εὐχολόγιον· χάρτης· ιη΄ × ιγ΄· φύλλα ρμη΄· μονόστηλον·
γραμμαὶ ιγ΄.

Prayers; paper; 18 × 13; 148 leaves; one column; 13
lines.

225

Ψαλτήριον· χάρτης· ις΄ × ιβ΄· φύλλα σξς΄· μονόστηλον·
γραμμαὶ ια΄.

Psalter; paper; 16 × 12; 266 leaves; one column; 11
lines.

226

Ὕμνοι· καὶ κανῶνες τῆς Ἐκκλησίας· χάρτης· ιζ΄ × ιβ΄·
φύλλα ϟη΄· μονόστηλον· γραμμαὶ ιβ΄· νεωτέρας ἐποχῆς.

Hymns, and Canons of the Church; paper; 17 × 12;
98 leaves; one column; 12 lines; late.

227

Εὐαγγέλια κατ᾽ ἀναγνώσεις· χάρτης· κβ΄ × ιγ΄· φύλλα
σμ΄· μονόστηλον· γραμμαὶ ις΄· νεωτέρας ἐποχῆς.

Lectionary; paper; 22 × 13; 240 leaves; one column;
16 lines; late.

228

Ἀπόστολος· χάρτης· ιδ΄ × ια΄· φύλλα σν΄· μονόστηλον·
γραμμαὶ ια΄· νεωτέρας ἐποχῆς.

Lectionary from the Acts and Epistles; paper; 14 × 11;
250 leaves; one column; 11 lines; late.

229

'Απόστολος· χάρτης· ἐλλειπὲς τὴν ἀρχήν· ιη' × ιγ'· φύλλα
σξα'· μονόστηλον· γραμμαὶ ις'· νεωτέρας ἐποχῆς.

Lectionary from the Acts and Epistles; paper; imperfect at the beginning; 18 × 13; 261 leaves; one column;
16 lines; late.

230

Τροπάριον· ܩܒܝܢ ܪܝܠܐ χάρτης· ιθ' × ιδ'·
φύλλα υλζ'· μονόστηλον· γραμμαὶ ιε'.

Troparion; paper; 19 × 14; 437 leaves; one column;
15 lines.

231

Τὰ Εὐαγγέλια· χάρτης· κα' × ιδ'· φύλλα σπη'· μονόστη-
λον· γραμμαὶ ιε'· νεωτέρας ἐποχῆς.

The Gospels; paper; 21 × 14; 288 leaves; one column;
15 lines; late.

232

Τροπάριον· χάρτης· κς' × ιζ'· φύλλα σνη'· μονόστηλον·
γραμμαὶ κ'· νεωτέρας ἐποχῆς.

Troparion; paper; 26 × 17; 258 leaves; one column;
20 lines; late.

233

Μηναῖον· χάρτης· κε' × ιζ'· φύλλα σοε'· μονόστηλον·
γραμμαὶ κ'.

Menæon; paper; 25 × 17; 275 leaves; one column;
20 lines.

234

Προφητολόγιον· χάρτης· ἐλλειπὲς τὴν ἀρχὴν δύο φύλλων·
κε΄ × ιζ΄· φύλλα ρλϛ΄· μονόστηλον· γραμμαὶ κδ΄· νεωτέρας
ἐποχῆς.

Prophetologion ; paper ; 2 leaves wanting at the beginning ; 25 × 17 ; 136 leaves ; one column ; 24 lines ; late.

235

'Ακολουθία· χάρτης· ἐλλειπὲς τὴν ἀρχὴν φύλλων δ΄·
κδ΄ × ιζ΄· φύλλα ροζ΄· δίστηλον· γραμμαὶ κα΄.

Service-book ; paper ; four leaves wanting at the beginning ; 24 × 17 ; 177 leaves ; two columns ; 21 lines.

236

Συναξάριον ἀπὸ τῶν Εὐαγγελίων· χάρτης· κα΄ × ιδ΄·
φύλλα τοη΄· μονόστηλον· γραμμαὶ ιζ΄· νεωτέρας ἐποχῆς.

Synaxarion from the Gospels ; paper ; 21 × 14 ; 378
leaves ; one column ; 17 lines ; late.

237

Μηναῖον· χάρτης· κα΄ × ιγ΄· φύλλα ροβ΄· μονόστηλον·
γραμμαὶ ιζ΄· νεωτέρας ἐποχῆς.

Menæon ; paper ; 21 × 13 ; 172 pages ; one column ;
17 lines ; late.

238

'Αναγνώσεις ἀπὸ τῶν Εὐαγγελίων· χάρτης· ιθ΄ × ιγ΄·
φύλλα τλβ΄· μονόστηλον· γραμμαὶ ιϛ΄· νεωτέρας ἐποχῆς.

Lectionary from the Gospels ; paper ; 19×13 ; 332 leaves ;
one column ; 16 lines ; late.

239

Εὐχολόγιον· χάρτης· ιθ' × ιγ'· φύλλα τκα'· μονόστηλον· γραμμαὶ ιδ'· νεωτέρας ἐποχῆς.

Prayers; paper; 19 × 13; 321 leaves; one column; 14 lines; late.

240

Ψαλτήριον· χάρτης· ιη' × ιβ'· φύλλα ρνγ'· μονόστηλον· γραμμαὶ ιδ'· νεωτέρας ἐποχῆς.

Psalter; paper; 18 × 12; 153 leaves; one column; 14 lines; late.

241

Ψαλτήριον· χάρτης· φύλλα ρνδ'.

Psalter; paper; 154 leaves.

242

Ψαλτήριον· ἐλλειπὲς τὴν ἀρχὴν ἑνὸς φύλλου· χάρτης· ιϛ' × ιβ'· φύλλα ρξδ'· μονόστηλον· γραμμαὶ ιε'· νεωτέρας ἐποχῆς.

Psalter; one leaf wanting at the beginning; paper; 16 × 12; 164 leaves; one column; 15 lines; late.

243

Πεντηκοστάριον· χάρτης· ιθ' × ιγ'· φύλλα ξδ'· μονόστη-λον· γραμμαὶ ιθ'· νεωτέρας ἐποχῆς· φύλλα τινὰ ἐν στρογ-γύλῃ συριακῇ καὶ ἐν συριακῇ τῆς Παλαιστίνης ἐν τῷ δεσίμῳ.

Pentecostarion; paper; 19 × 13; 64 leaves; one column; 19 lines; late. Some pages of Estrangelo and of Palestinian Syriac in the cover.

244

Ψαλτήριον· χάρτης· πολὺ διεφθαρμένον· ιδ' × ιβ'· μονό-στηλον· γραμμαὶ ιβ'· νεωτέρας ἐποχῆς.

Psalter; paper; much dilapidated; 14 × 12; one column; 12 lines; late.

245

Ψαλτήριον· χάρτης· ιε΄ × ι΄· φύλλα ρϟϛ΄· μονόστηλον· γραμμαὶ ιζ΄· νεωτέρας ἐποχῆς· ἐλλειπὲς φύλλων τινῶν τὴν ἀρχήν.

Psalter ; paper ; 15 × 10 ; 196 leaves ; one column ; 17 lines ; late ; a few leaves gone at the beginning.

246

Προσευχαί· ὀλίγα τετράδια· χάρτης· ιη΄ × ιδ΄· φύλλα κε΄· μονόστηλον· γραμμαὶ ιδ΄· νεωτέρας ἐποχῆς.

Prayers; a few quires only ; paper ; 18 × 14; 25 leaves; one column ; 14 lines ; late.

247

Ψαλτήριον· χάρτης· ιε΄ × ια΄· φύλλα ρι΄· μονόστηλον· γραμμαὶ ιβ΄.

Psalter ; paper ; 15 × 11 ; 110 leaves ; one column ; 12 lines.

248

Πεντηκοστάριον· χάρτης· ιδ΄ × η΄· φύλλα σνε΄· μονόστηλον· γραμμαὶ ιβ΄.

Pentecostarion ; paper; 14 × 8; 255 leaves; one column; 12 lines.

249

Λειτουργικά· ἐλλειπὲς τὴν ἀρχήν· χάρτης· ιε΄ × ια΄· φύλλα ριγ΄· μονόστηλον· γραμμαὶ ιγ΄.

Liturgical ; imperfect at the beginning; paper; 15 × 11 ; 113 leaves; one column ; 13 lines.

250

ܟܬܒܐ ܕܬܫܡܫܬܐ ܣܘܡܝܐ Λειτουργικά· χάρτης·
ιζ' × ιε'· φύλλα σιβ'· μονόστηλον· γραμμαὶ ιγ'.

Liturgical ; paper ; 17 × 15 ; 212 leaves ; one column ;
13 lines.

251

Λειτουργικά· χάρτης· ιδ' × ια'· φύλλα ρϟβ'· μονόστη-
λον· γραμμαὶ θ'.

Liturgical ; paper ; 14 × 11 ; 192 leaves ; one column ;
9 lines.

252

Πεντηκοστάριον· χάρτης· ιζ' × ια'· φύλλα ριζ'· μονό-
στηλον· γραμμαὶ ιγ'.

Pentecostarion ; paper ; 17 × 11 ; 117 leaves ; one
column ; 13 lines.

253

Ψαλτήριον· χάρτης· ιβ' × η'· φύλλα σζ'· μονόστηλον·
γραμμαὶ ιδ'.

Psalter ; paper ; 12 × 8 ; 207 leaves ; one column ; 14
lines.

254

Λειτουργικά· χάρτης· ιθ' × ιδ'· φύλλα νβ'· μονόστηλον·
γραμμαὶ ιϛ'.

Liturgical ; paper ; 19 × 14 ; 52 leaves ; one column ;
16 lines.

255

ܫܡܠ ܕܐܠܗܐ ܕܝܘܢ Λειτουργικά· χάρτης· ιγ' × ια'·
φύλλα ξη'· μονόστηλον· γραμμαὶ ια'.

Liturgical ; paper ; 13 × 11 ; 68 leaves ; one column ;
11 lines.

256

ܠܡܝܬܐ ܕܥܠ ܨܠܘܬܐ Εὐχαὶ διὰ τοὺς τεθνη-
κότας· χάρτης· ιγ' × θ'· φύλλα ρξθ'· μονόστηλον· γραμμαὶ ιγ'.

Prayers for the dead ; paper ; 13 × 9 ; 169 leaves ; one
column ; 13 lines.

257

Ψαλτήριον· ἐλλειπὲς τὴν ἀρχὴν καὶ τὸ τέλος· χάρτης·
ιϛ' × ιβ'· φύλλα ρλγ'· μονόστηλον· γραμμαὶ ιδ'.

Psalter ; imperfect at the beginning and end ; paper ;
16 × 12 ; 133 leaves ; one column ; 14 lines.

258

Εὐχολόγιον· ἐλλειπὲς τὴν ἀρχὴν δέκα φύλλων· χάρτης·
η' × ιβ'· φύλλα ρλϛ'· μονόστηλον· γραμμαὶ ιδ'.

Book of prayers ; ten leaves lost at the beginning ;
paper ; 8 × 12 ; 136 leaves ; one column ; 14 lines.

259

Εὐαγγέλια κατ' ἀναγνώσεις· χάρτης· κβ' × ιδ'· φύλλα
ρξ'· μονόστηλον· γραμμαὶ ιθ'.

Lectionary ; paper ; 22 × 14 ; 160 leaves ; one column ;
19 lines.

260

Ψαλτήριον· ἐλλειπές· χάρτης· ιϛ' × ιβ'· φύλλα ριζ'·
μονόστηλον· γραμμαὶ ια'.

Psalter ; imperfect ; paper ; 16 × 12 ; 117 leaves ; one
column ; 11 lines.

261

Λειτουργικά· ἐλλειπὲς τὴν ἀρχὴν φύλλων μα'· ιβ' × ιθ'·
φύλλα σνη'· μονόστηλον· γραμμαὶ ιγ'.

Liturgical; 41 leaves wanting at the beginning; 12 × 19;
258 leaves; one column; 13 lines.

262

Λειτουργικά· χάρτης· ις' × ια'· φύλλα πε'· μονόστηλον·
γραμμαὶ ιε'.

Liturgical; paper; 16 × 11; 85 leaves; one column;
15 lines.

263

Λειτουργικά· χάρτης· ιζ' × ιβ'· φύλλα ρλθ'· μονόστη-
λον· γραμμαὶ ιδ'.

Liturgical; paper; 17 × 12; 139 leaves; one column;
14 lines.

264

Ὡρολόγιον· χάρτης· ις' × ιβ'· φύλλα ϟη'· μονόστηλον·
γραμμαὶ ιβ'.

Horologion; paper; 16 × 12; 98 leaves; one column;
12 lines.

265

Λειτουργικά· χάρτης· ἐλλειπὲς τὴν ἀρχὴν καὶ τὸ τέλος·
χωρὶς δεσίμου· ις' × ιε'· φύλλα ιη'· μονόστηλον· γραμμαὶ
ιγ'.

Liturgical; imperfect at beginning and end; paper;
no cover; 16 × 15; 18 leaves; one column; 13 lines.

266

Λειτουργικά· χάρτης· κα' × ιγ'· φύλλα ιζ'· μονόστηλον·
γραμμαὶ ιζ'.

Liturgical; paper; 21 × 13; 17 leaves; one column;
17 lines.

267

Ψαλτήριον· χάρτης· ιγ' × η'· φύλλα σιη'· μονόστηλον· γραμμαὶ ιγ'· χωρὶς δεσίμου.

Psalter; paper; 13 × 8; 218 leaves; one column; 13 lines; binding lost.

268

Ψαλτήριον· χάρτης· ιβ' × η'· φύλλα τις'· μονόστηλον· γραμμαὶ θ'.

Psalter; paper; 12 × 8; 316 leaves; one column; 9 lines.

269

Συναξάριον τῶν Εὐαγγελίων διὰ τὸ ἔτος· χάρτης· κε' × ιη'· φύλλα ρξη'· δίστηλον· γραμμαὶ ιθ'.

Synaxarion of the Gospels for the whole year; paper; 25 × 18; 168 leaves; two columns; 19 lines.

270

Λειτουργικά· χάρτης· κβ' × ιδ'· φύλλα σξη'· μονόστη-λον· γραμμαὶ ις'.

Liturgical; paper; 22 × 14; 268 leaves; one column; 16 lines.

271

Συναξάριον ἀναγνώσεων ἀπὸ τῶν Εὐαγγελίων· χάρτης· κβ' × ιδ'· φύλλα ρξβ'· μονόστηλον· γραμμαὶ κ'.

Synaxarion of lessons from the Gospels; paper; 22 × 14; 162 leaves; one column; 20 lines.

272

Τὰ τέσσαρα Εὐαγγέλια· ἐλλειπὲς τὴν ἀρχὴν φύλλων ζ'· χωρὶς δεσίμου· χάρτης· κϛ' × ιη'· φύλλα ρο'· δίστηλον· γραμμαὶ κ'.

Four Gospels; 7 leaves wanting at the beginning; no cover; paper; 26 × 18; 170 leaves; two columns; 20 lines.

273

Εἱρμολόγιον· χάρτης· ιδ × ι· φύλλα σθ· μονόστηλον· γραμμαὶ ιβ'.

Hirmologion; paper; 14 × 10; 209 leaves; one column; 12 lines.

274

Στιχηράριον· χάρτης· ιϛ' × ιβ'· φύλλα ρν· μονόστηλον· γραμμαὶ η'· ἐλλειπές.

Sticherarion; paper; 16 × 12; 150 leaves; one column; 8 lines; imperfect.

275

Ψαλτήριον· χάρτης· ιδ' × η'· φύλλα σιζ'· μονόστηλον· γραμμαὶ ιβ'.

Psalter; paper; 14 × 8; 217 leaves; one column; 12 lines.

276

Λειτουργικά· χάρτης· ιγ' × η'· φύλλα σλδ'· μονόστηλον· γραμμαὶ ια'.

Liturgical; paper; 13 × 8; 234 leaves; one column; 11 lines.

PLATE IV.

Palestinian Syriac Lectionary. No. 1. A.D. 1094.

To face page 93.

PLATE V.

Palestinian Syriac Lectionary.   No. 2.   A.D. 1098.

To face page 93.

PLATE VI.

Palestinian Syriac Lectionary.   From the cover of No. 1.

To face page 93.

ΕΝ ΣΥΡΙΑΚΗι ΤΗΣ ΠΑΛΑΙΣΤΙΝΗΣ.

PALESTINIAN SYRIAC.

1

Εὐαγγέλια κατ᾽ ἀναγνώσεις· μεμβράνη· κδ᾽ × ιη᾽ ἑκατο-
στόμετρα· φύλλα ρν᾽· δίστηλον· τοῦ ἔτους ‚αϟδ᾽· γραφὴ
σαφὴς καὶ ὡραία. φύλλα δι᾽ ἄλλου χειρογράφου εἰς τὸ τέλος,
μετ᾽ ἀναγνώσεων ἀπὸ Ἰωάννου ια᾽, ιβ᾽, ιδ᾽, ιζ᾽, ιϛ᾽. Ἐν τῷ
δεσίμῳ ὑπάρχει φύλλον μετ᾽ ἀναγνώσεως περιεχούσης τοὺς
τελευταίους στίχους Ἰωάννου ζ, τοὺς στίχους α᾽ καὶ β᾽
Ἰωάννου η᾽, καὶ τὴν ἀρχὴν Ἰωάννου ια᾽.

Lectionary on vellum; 24 cm. × 18; 150 leaves; two
columns; date A.D. 1094; fine distinct writing. There are
four leaves from another lectionary at the end, with read-
ings from John xi. xii. xiv. xvii. xvi. In the cover is
another leaf containing the last verses of John vii. and
the first two verses of John viii.; also the beginning of
John xi.

2

Εὐαγγέλια κατ᾽ ἀναγνώσεις· μεμβράνη· κβ᾽ × ιϛ᾽· φύλλα
ρμγ᾽· δίστηλον· τοῦ ἔτους ‚αϟη᾽. Εἰς τὸ τέλος εἰσὶ δύο
φύλλα στρογγύλου συριακοῦ.

Lectionary on vellum; 22 × 16; 143 leaves; two columns;
date A.D. 1098. There are two leaves of Estrangelo Syriac
at the end.

3

Ἀποσπάσματα ὁμιλιῶν τινων ἐν τῷ δεσίμῳ ἀραβικοῦ
βιβλίου εὑρεθέντα· μεμβράνη· κα᾽ × ιε᾽· φύλλα ιδ᾽· δίστη-
λον· τῆς ἑνδεκάτης ἑκατονταετηρίδος.

Fragments of discourses found in the cover of an Arabic
book; vellum; 21½ × 15; 14 leaves; two columns; cent. XI.

APPENDIX.

ΑΠΟΣΠΑΣΜΑΤΑ
ΤΑ ΠΛΕΙΣΤΑ ΕΛΛΗΝΙΚΑ

FRAGMENTS, CHIEFLY GREEK.

1

Τὰ ἀποσπάσματα Βρύγσχ.

Λευιτικὸν κβ′	γ′—η′	Leviticus xxii.	3—8
κβ′	θ′—ιδ′	xxii.	9—14
κβ′	ιϛ′—κα′	xxii.	16—21
κβ′	κα′—κζ′	xxii.	21—27
κβ′	κη′—κγ′ γ′	xxii.	28—xxiii. 3
κγ′	ϛ′—ιβ′	xxiii.	6—12
κγ′	ιβ′—ιζ′	xxiii.	12—17
κγ′	ιζ′—κβ′	xxiii.	17—22

Κεφαλαιώδεσι γράμμασιν· κβ′ × ιϛ′· φύλλα β′· δίστη-λον· γραμμαὶ λα′.

Uncials; 22 cm. × 16; 2 leaves; two columns; 31 lines.

These fragments were first published by Brugsch, but incorrectly described as new fragments of the Codex Sinaiticus. They were reprinted, by Harris, from Brugsch, with a few corrections. They constitute No. 15 in *Biblical Fragments from Mount Sinai.*

Other corrections to Brugsch should be made as follows:

Fol. 1 recto, col. 1, line 11. *For* λεπρος *read* λεπραν

Fol. 1 recto, col. 2, line 28. The initial κ should be extended on the margin, and so in l. 30

Fol. 1 verso, col. 2, line 2. *Add* a point after τω, and so after үмιn in l. 28

Fol. 2 recto, col. 2, lines 20, 21. *Transfer* тo at the beginning of l. 21 to l. 20

Fol. 2 recto, col. 2, lines 26, 27. *Transfer* ιερεγс from l. 27 to l. 26

Fol. 2 verso, col. 1, lines 8, 9. *Add* ειν at the end of l. 8 ; and *remove* ιn from the beginning of l. 9

line 15 *for* ειстасгενεас *read* νομιμον...

line 16 *read* ...ειстасгενεас

line 17 *erase* ιονεν

line 19 *erase* final ν

line 26 *for* εβΔομηс *read* нмερας

Fol. 2 verso, col. 2, line 6. *For* βογκωλιον *read* βογκολιον

line 27 *erase* final ειс

2

Ἄλλοτε ἦτο ἓν φύλλον, ἀλλ᾽ ἐσπάσθη. Καὶ τώρα τὰ δύο μέρη εἰσι συγκεκολλημένα ὥστε μέρος τι τοῦ μείζονος μέρους καλύπτεται διὰ τοῦ μείονος. Τὸ δὲ κείμενόν ἐστι ἀπὸ Κριτῶν κ΄.

Τὸ χειρόγραφον ἦτο τοὐλάχιστον δίστηλον· ἑκάστη στήλη εἶχε τοὐλάχιστον γραμμὰς κζ΄. Τὰ δὲ φύλλα εἰσὶν ἀτελῆ. Κεφαλαιώδεσι γράμμασιν. μέγεθος ἑκατοστόμετρα κϛ΄ × ζ΄.

This was once one leaf, but it has been torn, and now the two pieces are glued together, so that part of the larger piece is covered by the smaller. The text is from Judges xx.

The manuscript had at least two columns to the page. Each column had at least 27 lines. The leaves are imperfect. It is written in uncials. The size is 10 inches by 3[1].

[1] This is No. 2 in Rendel Harris' *Biblical Fragments*.

3

Συνίσταται ἐκ δύο μερῶν κεφαλαιώδους χειρογράφου ἐπὶ
τεμάχιον ξύλου κεκολλημένων, ὥστε ἀναγιγνώσκομεν αὐτὰ εἰς
ἓν μέρος μόνον.

Τὸ χειρόγραφον εἶχε, φαίνεται, τοὐλάχιστον δύο στήλας.
ἦσαν γραμμαὶ μγ´ ἐν μιᾷ τῶν σελίδων. Ἡ δὲ γραφὴ ὁμοιά-
ζεται τῇ τοῦ ἀρίθ. β´. Τὸ κείμενόν ἐστι τὸ αὐτό, δηλαδὴ
ἀπὸ τῶν Κριτῶν, καὶ ἀπὸ Ῥούθ. Διὰ τοῦτο νομίζομεν ὅτι
ἀμφότεροί ἐστιν μέρη ἑνὸς χειρογράφου.

Κεφαλαιώδεσι γράμμασιν· κδ´ × ιδ´.

This consists of two pieces of a leaf, written in uncials,
glued on to a piece of wood, so that it can be read on one
side only.

The manuscript seems to have had at least two columns
to the page. There were 43 lines to the page. The writing
resembles that of No. 2. The text is the same, from the
Book of Judges and from Ruth. For this reason we suspect
that both are parts of the same manuscript.

Uncials; 24 centimetres by 14[1].

4

Μικρὸν τεμάχιον ξύλου ἀφ᾽ ἑνὸς δεσίμου μετ᾽ ἀποσπά-
σματος μεμβράνης, πιθανὸν τοῦ ἕκτου αἰῶνος.

ιδ´ × γ´. φύλλα τινὰ νεωτέρας ἐποχῆς ἐκ μεμβράνης εὑρί-
σκονται ἐν τῷ αὐτῷ φακέλλῳ.

A small piece of wood[2] from a binding with a bit of
vellum on it, perhaps as early as the sixth century.

14 cm. × 3. A few later pieces of vellum are in the
same packet.

---

[1] No. 3 in *Biblical Fragments*.
[2] This is No. 7 in *Biblical Fragments*.

5

Μικρὸν τεμάχιον μεμβράνης, πολὺ λεπτόν, ἀπὸ τοῦ δεσίμου ἑνὸς βιβλίου, ἴσως τοῦ πέμπτου αἰῶνος. ιδ΄ × ϛ΄.

A tiny fragment of vellum, very thin, from the cover of
a book, perhaps of the fifth century. 14 cm. × 6.

The side of it which is legible contains a part of two
verses from the xiiith chapter of Acts as follows:

Acts xiii. 28, 29.

```
. . . . . TO . . . . .
. . . . HT . . . . .
πειλατον αναιρ
εθηναι αυτον ως
δε ετελεσαν              5
παντα τα περι
αυτου γεγραμ
μενα καθελοντες
. . . απο του ξυλου
. . . . εθηκαν εις       10
μνημιον· ο δε
θ̄ϲ αυτὸν ηγει
ρεν εκ νεκρων
οσ ωφθη επι ημε
ρασ πλιους              15
τοισ συναναβα
σιν αυτω απο
```

6

Ἀποσπάσματα χειρογράφου, ἐν συριακῇ τῆς Παλαι-
στίνης· τὸ κείμενόν ἐστιν ἐκ τῆς ἐπιστολῆς πρὸς τοὺς
Γαλάτας. κδ΄ × ιϛ΄· φύλλα δ΄.

Palestinian Syriac fragments, from Galatians, the same
as in *Sinai Fragments*, No. 16, but with an additional
double leaf.

24 cm. × 16; four leaves.

Correct the text in *Sinai Fragments* as follows: in fol.
1 verso, col. 2, l. 11. *For* ܪܩܘܙܠܐ *read* ܪܩܘܙܠܗ and
observe that some letters can be read of col. 1, e.g.

ܐ	line 9 being in rubric as the commencement of a new chapter.
ܘܪ	
ܩܘ	
ܘܗܐ	
ܒܣ 5	
ܬ	
ܪ	
ــــــــــ	
ܐ/	
ܐ 10	
ܘܠܐ	
ܘܝ	
ܘܝ̈	
ܝ̇	
ܠܫܝ 15	
ܘܣ	

Fol. 2 recto, col. 1, l. 10. *For* ܠܝ *read* ܠܝ̇.

The new pages are as follows:

Fol. 3 recto.

Col. *b*	Col. *a*
Gal. ii. 17—	Gal. ii. 15—17.
ܐ......	ܕܛܠ ܣܘܐܪܐ
ܘܝ......	ܘܠܐ ܡܢ ܥܡܠܐ
ܐܫ......	ܣܡܠܩ܀ ܕܝܬܡ̇ܐ
ܐܘ......	ܕܠܐ ܐܚܝ ܡܢܕ ܕܝܪܫ
ܣܩ......	ܡܢ ܩܘܐܝܘ

13—2

......	
......	
......	
......	Rubric
......	
......	
......	
......	
......	
......	
......	

Fol. 3 verso.

Col. *b*	Col. *a*
Gal. iii. 1—3.	Gal. ii.
....	....
	....
	....
	......
(! sic)	......
	......
	......
	......
	......
	......

ܕܢܡܘܣܐ ܢܣܒܬܘܢ	ܘܪ̇......
ܪ̇ܘܚܐ ܐܘ̇	ܕܝ ܀......
ܡܢ ܡܫܡܥܘܬܗ̇	ܐ......
ܕܗܝܡܢܘܬܐ ܀	ܠܗܐ......
ܗܟܢ ܠܝܬ ܒܟܘܢ	ܒ......
...... ܫܪ̈ܝܬܘܢ	ܘܐ......

Fol. 4 recto.

Col. *b*	Col. *a*
Gal. iii. 8—	Gal. iii. 5—7.
....	......ܘܐܝܟ...
....	......ܕܡܫܦܪ̇
....	......ܪ̇ܘܚܐ
ܡܢ......	ܘܡܥܒܕ ܒܟܘܢ
ܗܘܐ......	ܚ̈ܝܠܐ ܡܢ ܥܒ̈ܕܘܗܝ
ܕܡܢ......	ܕܢܡܘܣܐ. ܐܘ̇
ܡܛ......	ܡܢ ܡܫܡܥܘܬܐ
ܡܣ......	ܕܗܝܡܢܘܬܐ
ܒܗܠ......	ܗܝܟ ܕܟܬܝܒ
ܡܢ......	ܕܗܝܡܢ ܐܒܪܗܡ
ܕܝ......	ܠܐܠܗܐ. ܘܐܬܚܫܒܬ
ܠܘܦ......	ܠܗ ܠܙܕܝܩܘ ܀
ܒܬܒ......	ܗܘܘ ܐܘ̇ ܝܕ̈ܥܝܢ
ܗܘ......	ܕܐܝܠܝܢ ܕܡܢ
ܡܛܠ......	ܗܝܡܢܘܬܐ ܗܢܘܢ
....	ܒܢ̈ܘܗܝ ܕܐܒܪܗܡ

Fol. 4 verso.

Col. *b*	Col. *a*
Gal. iii. 14—16.	Gal. iii. . .—14
ܠܓܠܠ ܕܡܫܝܚܐ	......ܒܙ
ܪܘܚܐ ܢܣܒ	......ܒܠܐ
ܒܬܪܟܗ ܕܗܝܡܢܘܬܐ	......ܦ
ܐܚܝܐ ܕܒܪܢܫ	......ܗ
ܐܢܐ ܐܡܪ ܀	......ܐ ܀
ܒܪܢ ܕܝ ܕܡܬܩܝܡ	......ܠܝܬ
ܕܒܪܢܫ ܕܗܘܝܐ	......ܘܠ
ܡܫܪܪܐ. ܐܢܫ	......ܕ
ܠܐ ܡܣܠܝ ܠܗ. ܐܘ	......ܗܘܢ ܀
ܡܘܣܦ ܠܗܘܒܠܗ ܀	Rubric ......
ܠܐܒܪܗܡ ܕܝ	......ܬܢ
ܐܬܐܡܪܝ ܡܫܘܝܬܐ	......ܒܘܬܐ :
ܘܠܙܪܥܗ ܀ ܠܐ	......ܒܪ
ܐܡܪ ܠܙܪܥܝܬܢ	......ܘܦ
ܗܝ ܕܥܠ ܣܓܝ	......ܠܦ
ܐܠܐ ܗܝܢ ܕܥܠ	......ܬܠ

7

[1]Δύο φύλλα χειρογράφου τῶν Εὐαγγελίων τοῦ ἕκτου αἰῶνος, οὗ τὸ μὲν πρῶτον δεῖται τοῦ ἄνω μέρους. Τὸ δὲ δεύτερον πτυχθὲν ὑπὸ τινὸς διὰ νὰ χρησιμεύῃ εἰς τὸ δέσιμον ἄλλου βιβλίου, ἐγένετο δυσανάγνωστον ὅπου ἐπτύχθη. Ἡ

[1] No. 11 in *Biblical Fragments.*

PLATE VII.

Fragment of St Mark's Gospel.   Appendix No. 8.

γραφή ἐστι μεγάλη καὶ σαφής· ὄντος τοῦ χειρογράφου ἀφ'
οὗ ἐσπάσθησαν τὰ τεμάχια ὡραίου σφόδρα.

Two leaves of a sixth century MS. of the Gospels, the
first of the leaves having lost its upper half. The second
leaf, having been folded in the middle when used to bind
some other MS., has become illegible where it was folded.
The hand is a large bold script, and the MS. from which
the fragments came must have been a very fine one.

8

Τρία ἀποσπάσματα παναρχαίου χειρογράφου τῶν Εὐαγγελίων. Ἡ γραφή ἐστι περίεργος, σχεδὸν κεφαλαιώδης. Ἡ
μεμβράνη ἐστι πολὺ τετριμμένη. κβ′ × ις′.

[1]Three fragments of a very ancient manuscript of the
Gospels of the seventh (?) century. Of the three leaves
two are stuck together. 22 cm. × 16.

The importance of these fragments lies (i) palæographi-
cally in the fact that they are written in a curious Coptic
half-uncial, not unlike the hand of the famous Codex
Marchalianus of the prophets; and (ii) critically in their
containing the concluding verses of St Mark's Gospel in
the form of a double alternative known to us from Codex
L. These verses are only legible by holding the compacted
leaves in strong sunlight, when the inside writing becomes
visible. In this way we transcribe the following verses:

Col. 1	Col. 2
ιδε ο τοπος οπου	ΤΑΥΤΑ ΚΑΙ ΑΥΤΟС
εθηκαν αυτον	ΙC ΑΠΟ ΑΝΑΤΟΛΗС
αλλα υπαγετε ειπα	ΑΧΡΙ ΔΥСΕѠС ΕẐΑ
τε τοις μαθηταις αυ	ΠΕСΤΕΙΛΕΝ ΔΙ ΑΥ
του και τω πετρω	ΤѠΝ ΤΟ ΙΕΡΟΝ ΚΑΙ
οτι προαγει υμας	ΑΦΘΑΡΤΟΝ ΚΗΡΥ
εις την γαλιλαιαν	ΓΜΑ ΤΗС ΑΙѠΝΙΟΥ

[1] No. 12 in *Sinai Fragments.*

εκει αυτον οψεσθε   ϲωτηριαϲ ᴀμην[1]

καθως ειπεν υμῑ   εϲτιν ᴅε κᴀι τᴀγτᴀ

και εξελθογϲᴀι εφγ   φερομενᴀ μετᴀ

γον απο τογ мνн   το εφοβογντο ᴦᴀρ

μειου ειχεν ᴦᴀρ ᴀγ   ᴀνᴀϲτᴀϲ ᴅε πρωϊ

ταϛ τρομοϲ κᴀι εκ   πρωτн ϲᴀββᴀτογ

στασις και ογᴅεν   εφᴀνн πρωτον

ι ουδεν ειπον εφο   мᴀριᴀ тн мᴀᴦᴅᴀ

βουντο γαρ z z z z   лнνн πᴀρ нϲ

           z z z z   εκβεβлнκει επτᴀ

           z z z z   ᴅᴀιмονιᴀ εκεινн

ευαγγελιο͞ν   πορεγθ . . . ᴀπнᴦ

κατα μαρκον   ᴦειлεν . . . ме

We can also read some more letters from the portions of the previous pages which have been folded together as follows:

Fol. 2 verso.

Col. 1

· · · · · · · · · ·

πᴀρεϲτнκεν εξ̅ ε

ναντιαϛ ᴀγτογ οτι

ουτως εκραξεν

ειπεν ᴀлнθωϲ

ουτοϛ γ͞ϲ θ͞γ н̅

нϲαν δε και ᴦγνᴀι

κεϛ απο μακροθεν

θεωρουσαι εν ᴀιϲ

και μαρια н мᴀ

ᴦδαληνη κᴀι мᴀ

ρια η ιακωβογ τογ

Col. 2

· · · · · · · · · ·

· · · · · · · · · ·

βογлεγтнϲ οϲ κᴀι

ᴀγτοϲ нν προϲ ᴅε

χομενοϲ тнν βᴀϲι

лειᴀν τογ θ͞γ τοл

мнϲᴀϲ ειϲнлθεν

προϲ πιлᴀτον και

нтнϲᴀτο το ϲωмᴀ

τογ ι͞γ

ο̅ ᴅε πιлᴀτοϲ εθᴀγ

мᴀϲεν ε . . . . .

end of leaf.

---

[1] The next three lines are in a smaller character.

9

Ἓν φύλλον παναρχαίου διγλώσσου κεφαλαιώδους χειρογράφου τῶν Εὐαγγελίων. Ἐστὶ πολὺ ἐνδιαφέρον, διότι ἐστι
τυχὸν τὸ ἀρχαιότατον παράδειγμα ἀραβικῆς μεταφράσεως
τῆς Νέας Διαθήκης.

[1]One leaf of a very old bilingual manuscript of the
Gospels, in Greek and Arabic. It is most interesting, be-
cause it is perhaps the oldest known specimen of an Arabic
version of the New Testament.

As there are some errors in the transcription of the
Arabic portion of these pages in *Biblical Fragments*, and
more of the text can be read than is there printed, I
have re-transcribed it.

Verso	Recto
Col. 2	Col. 2
Matt. xiii. 49—52.	Matt. xiii. 46—48.

. . . . .	. . . . .
هكذا	كثير الثمن
يكون في انقضا،	فباع [ن]هب
هذا العالم	شي له . . . . . .
تخرج الملا	اشتراها . . . . . .
يكة فيفرزون	[ا]يضا يشبه . . .
الاشرار من بين	السموات . . . . .
الصديقين	كة. . . . .
و يلقوهم	كل . . . .
في قامين	في البحر . . . .
نار	ناس جمعت . .
هناك يكون	امتلات . . . . . .

[1] No. 9 in *Sinai Fragments*.

البكا و صرير ..... صعدوا
الاسنان .. علي الشطر
و قال لهم يسوع ..... جلسوا
فهمتم هذا كله ..... فاختاروا
فقالوا ..... في انية
له نعم يا[رب] والاشرار برا طرحوا
و هو قال لهم

10

Δέκα φύλλα παλιμψήστου χειρογράφου τῶν Εὐαγγελίων ἐν ᾧ ἡ ἀρχαία ἑλληνικὴ γραφὴ τοῦ πέμπτου αἰῶνος ὑπο-χωρεῖται εἰς συριακὸν κείμενον.

μέγεθος κϛ' × κ'.

Ten leaves of a palimpsest manuscript of the Gospels, in which the ancient Greek writing is covered by a Syriac text[1]. Size 26 cm. × 20.

Τὸ κείμενόν ἐστι·

Ματθαίου κε' ιε'—κα'	Matthew xxv.	15—21
,, κα'—κϛ'	,,	21—26
,, . κϛ'—λβ'	,,	26—32
,, λβ'—λζ'	,,	32—37
,, λζ'—μγ'	,,	37—43
,, μγ'—κϛ' β'	,,	43—xxvi. 2
κϛ' ιζ'—κγ'	xxvi.	17—23
,, κγ'—κη'	,,	23—28
,, κη'—λγ'	,,	28—33
,, λγ'—λθ'	,,	33—39
κη' ια'—ιζ	xxviii.	11—17
,, ιη'—τέλος	,,	18—fin.

[1] This is No. 10 of *Biblical Fragments*.

Μάρκου	α΄	ια΄—ιζ΄	Mark	i.	11—17
	,,	ιζ΄—κβ΄		,,	17—22
	β΄	κα΄—κε΄		ii.	21—25
	,,	κε΄—γ΄ γ΄		,,	25—iii. 3
	γ΄	κζ΄—λβ΄		iii.	27—32
	,,	λβ΄—δ΄ δ΄		,,	32—iv. 4
	ε΄	θ΄—ιε΄		v.	9—15
	,,	ιε΄—κ΄		,,	15—20

In *Biblical Fragments from Mount Sinai* nine leaves only were transcribed: an additional leaf has since come to light, which is transcribed below. Note that in the pages already published, on fol. 4ᵃ, col. 2, line 1 for ΥΜΩΝ we must read ΥΜΕΙC.

Fol. 10 recto.

Col. 1

Matt. xxv. 37—40.

H ΔΙΨΩΝΤΑ
ΚΑΙ ΕΠΟΤΙCΑ
ΜΕΝ · ΠΟΤΕ
ΔΕ CΕ ΕΙΔΟΜΕ̄
ΞΕΝΟΝ ΚΑΙ ΕΙC
ΗΓΑΓΟΜΕΝ
H ΓΥΜΝΟΝ
ΚΑΙ ΠΕΡΙΕΒΑ
ΛΟΜΕΝ ΠΟΤΕ
ΔΕ CΕ ΕΙΔΟΜΕ̄
ΑCΘΕΝΗ H Ε̄
ΦΥΛΑΚΗ ΚΑΙ
ΗΛΘΟΜΕΝ
ΠΡΟC CΕ · ΚΑΙ
ΑΠΟΚΡΙΘΕΙC
Ο ΒΑCΙΛΕΥC
ΕΡΕΙ ΑΥΤΟΙC

Col. 2

Matt. xxv. 40—43.

ΑΤΕ ΤΟΤΕ ΕΡΕΙ
ΤΟΙC ΕΞ ΕΥΩ̄
ΥΜΩΝ . . . . .
ΤΕ ΑΠ ΕΜΟΥ ΟΙ
ΚΑΤΗΡΑΜΕΝΟΙ
ΕΙC ΤΟ ΠΥΡ ΤΟ
ΔΙΩΝΙΟΝ ΤΟ
ΗΤΟΙΜΑCΜΕ
ΝΟΝ ΤΩ ΔΙΑΒΟ
ΛΩ ΚΑΙ ΤΟΙC
ΑΓΓΕΛΟΙC ΑΥ
ΤΟΥ ΕΠΙΝΑCΑ
ΓΑΡ ΚΑΙ ΟΥΚ Ε
ΔΩΚΑΤΑΙ ΜΟΙ
ΦΑΓΕΙΝ ΕΔΙ
ΨΗCΑ ΚΑΙ ΟΥ
Κ ΕΠΟΤΙCΑΤΑΙ

ΑΜΗΝ ΛΕΓω
ΥΜΙΝ ΕΦ Ο
CΟΝ ΕΠΟΙΗ
CΑΤΑΙ ΕΝΙ ΤΟΥ
ΤΟΥΤωΝ Α
ΔΕΛΦωΝ ΜΟΥ
ΤωΝ ΕΛΑΧΙCΤω̄
ΕΜΟΙ ΕΠΟΙΗC

ΜΕ · ΖΕΝΟC Η
ΜΗΝ ΚΑΙ ΟΥ
CΥΝΗΓΑΓΕΤΕ
ΜΕ · ΓΥΜΝΟC
ΚΑΙ ΟΥ ΠΕΡΙΕΒΑ
[1]ΚΑΤΑΙ ΜΕ ΑCΘΕ
ΝΗC ΚΑΙ ΕΝ ΦΥ
ΛΑΚΗ ΚΑΙ ΟΥΚ Ε

Fol. 10 verso.

Matt. xxv. 43—45.

ΠΕCΚΕΨΑC
ΜΕ · ΤΟΤΕ Α
ΠΟΚΡΙΘΗC Ο̄
ΤΑΙ ΚΑΙ ΑΥΤΟΙ
ΛΕΓΟΝΤΕC ·
Κ̄Ε̄ ΠΟΤΕ CΕ
ΕΙΔΟΜΕΝ ΠΙ
ΝωΝΤΑ Η ΔΙ
ΨωΝΤΑ · Η Ζ̄Ε
ΝΟΝ Η ΓΥΜΝΟ̄
Η ΑCΘΕΝΗ Η
ΕΝ ΦΥΛΑΚΗ.
ΚΑΙ ΟΥ ΔΙΗΚΟ
ΝΗCΑΜΕΝ CΟΙ
ΤΟΤΕ ΑΠΟΚΡΙ
ΘΗCΕΤΑΙ ΑΥ
ΤΟΙC ΛΕΓωΝ
ΑΜΗΝ ΛΕΓω
ΥΜΙΝ ΕΦ Ο
CΟΝ ΟΥΚ ΕΠΟ⌐Ι⌐

Matt. xxv. 46—xxvi. 2.

ΚΑΙ ΑΠΕΛΕΥ
CΟΝΤΑΙ ΟΥΤΟΙ
ΕΙC ΚΟΛΑCΙΝ
ΑΙωΝΙΟΝ ΟΙ
ΔΕ ΔΙΚΑΙΟΙ ΕΙC
ΖωΗΝ ΑΙωΝΙ
ΟΝ · ΚΑΙ ΕΓΕ
ΝΕΤΟ ΟΤΕ Ε
ΤΕΛΕCΕΝ Ο ῙC̄
ΠΑΝΤΑC ΤΟΥC
ΛΟΓΟΥC ΤΟΥ
ΤΟΥC ΕΙΠΕΝ
ΤΟΙC ΜΑΘΗΤΑΙC
ΑΥΤΟΥ ΟΙΔΑ
ΤΑΙ ΟΤΙ ΜΕΤΑ
ΔΥΟ ΗΜΕΡΑC
ΤΟ ΠΑCΧΑ ΓΙΝΕ
ΤΑΙ ΚΑΙ Ο ῩΙΟC
ΤΟΥ ΑΝΘΡω
ΠΟΥ ΠΑΡΑΔΙ

[1] ΚΑΤΑΙ for ΛΕΤΑΙ, the eye of the scribe wandering to the previous line.

ΗϹΑΤΕ ΕΝΙ ΤΟΥ

ΤΩΝ ΤΩΝ Ε

ΛΑΧΙϹΤΩΝ ΟΥ

ΔΕ ΕΜΟΙ ΕΠΟΙ

ΗϹΑΤΑΙ.

ΔΟΤΑΙ ΕΙϹ ΤΟ

ϹΤΑΥΡΩΘΗ

ΝΑΙ

ΤΟΤΕ ϹΥΝΗ

ΧΘΗϹΑΝ ΟΙ Δ

11

Τέσσαρα φύλλα ἐν κεφαλαιώδεσι γράμμασιν ἐκ τοῦ Εὐαγγελίου Ματθαίου ιγ'· ιδ'· ιε'·

κϛ' × ιη'· τοῦ ὀγδόου αἰῶνος.

[1]Four leaves, in uncials, from the Gospel of Matthew. Chaps. xiii. xiv. xv.

26 cm. × 18 ; eighth century.

12

Πέντε φύλλα ἐκ χειρογράφου τῶν Εὐαγγελίων κατ' ἀναγνώσεις· γραφὴ σαφὴς καὶ ὡραία καὶ πλαγία. κα' × ιη'.

Five leaves of a lectionary; very bold writing, slightly inclined. 21 cm. × 18.

13

Δύο φύλλα ἐκ χειρογράφου Εὐαγγελίων κατ' ἀναγνώσεις· γραφὴ σαφὴς καὶ ὡραία. δίστηλον· λα' × κγ'.

Two leaves of a lectionary in fine vertical uncials, two columns. 31 cm. × 23.

14

Ἕξ φύλλα ἐκ χειρογράφου Εὐαγγελίων κατ' ἀναγνώσεις ἐν λοξίοις κεφαλαιώδεσι γράμμασιν. κδ' × ιη'· μονόστηλον· γραμμαὶ ιη'. τοῦ δεκάτου αἰῶνος.

Six leaves of a lectionary in sloping uncials. 24 cm. × 18. One column ; 18 lines ; tenth century.

[1] No. 8 in *Sinai Fragments*.

15

Δύο φύλλα ὡραίου χειρογράφου Εὐαγγελίων κατ᾽ ἀναγνώσεις ἐν γραφῇ κεφαλαιώδει, μετ᾽ ἀναγνωστικῶν σημειώσεων
ἐν ἐρυθροῖς γράμμασι διὰ κομψῶν ἀρκτικῶν κεκοσμημένα.
κη΄ × κβ΄. δίστηλον· γραμμαὶ ιθ΄.

Two leaves of a fine lectionary in vertical uncials,
with red notes for reading. Pretty ornamented initials.
28 cm. × 22. Two columns; 19 lines.

16

Ἀποσπάσματά τινα ἀπ᾽ Εὐαγγελίων κατ᾽ ἀναγνώσεις τοῦ
ἐννάτου αἰῶνος.

A number of fragments of a lectionary of the ninth
century.

17

Ἀπόσπασμα τοῦ βίου τοῦ Ἁγίου Σαβᾶ, γραφέντος διὰ
τοῦ Ἁγίου Κυρίλλου τῆς Σκυθοπόλεως.

A fragment of the life of St Saba, by St Cyril of
Scythopolis (Cotelier, *Monumenta* iii. p. 241).

e.g.   ἐιс

MIMHCIN, ΦΗCΆΝΤΑ . ΜΆΘΕ
ΤΕ ἀπ᾽ ΕΜΟῦ . ΟΤΙ ΠΡΑῢC ἐι
ΜΙ ΚΑΙ ΤΑΠΕΙΝΟС ΤΗ ΚΑΡΔΙΑ·
ΠΡΟC ὅΠΕΡ ὙΠΟΔΕΙΓΜΑ ΒΛΕ
ΠΩΝ ΚΑΙ ὁ ΗΓΙΑCΜΕΝΟC Π̅Η̅Ρ̅
ΗΜῶΝ CΆΒΑС . ἘΤΑΠΕΙΝΟΥ

. . . .

Cf. with this fragment 28.

18

Ἀπόσπασμα ὁμιλίας τινός· δίστηλον· τοῦ ἐννάτου αἰῶνος.

Fragment of a homily in two columns; ninth century.
The text of this fragment is as follows:

Recto

Col. *a*

.... τὸ τὸ κρατος
.... ϲτυχηϲ περιϲτη
.... ωϲ δε ϲοι ἡ ἀ
κριβηϲ ἑαυτοῦ κα
τα νόηϲιϲ · αὐταρ
κη παρεξει χειρα
γωγιαν καὶ πρὸϲ τῆ
ἔννοιαν του θΥ ·
Ἐὰν γαρ προϲέχηϲ ϲε
αὐτῶ · ὐ̓δεν δεη
ϲει ἐκ τῆϲ τῶν ὅλω
καταϲκευῆϲ τὸν
δΙΜΙουργὸΝ ἐξι
χνευειν · ἀλλ εν ϲε
αυτῶ · οἱονὶ μικρῶ
τινι διακόϲμω
την μεγάλην κα
τόψει · τοῦ κτήϲαν
τόϲ ϲε ϲοφίαν · ἀϲω
ΜΑτον εννόει τον
θΝ · ἐκ τῆϲ ἐνΥπαρ
χουϲηϲ ϲοι ΨΥχηϲ
ἀϲωμάτου · μη πε
ριγραφόμενον τό
πω · ἐπειδὴ ὀΥδε ὁ ϲὸϲ

Verso

Col. *b*

ϲαντοϲ · προϲ ...
Εἰ δοκει μετα τη ...
τῆϲ ΨΥχῆϲ ... εωρ ..
αν καὶ τῆ τοῦ ϲώ
ΜΑτοϲ καταϲκεΥ
Η · καὶ θάΥΜΑϲΟΝ,
ὅπωϲ πρέπων ἀΥ
τῷ καταγωγιον
τῆ λογικῆ ΨΥχῆ.
ὁ ἀριϲτοτεχνηϲ ἐ
δηΜΙουργηϲεν ·
ὄρθιον ἔπλαϲε μό
νον τῶν ζῶων
τον ΑΝΟΝ · ἵνα ἐ
ξ ἀΥτοῦ τοῦ ϲχή
ΜΑτοϲ ἐίδηϲ ὅτι
. . . .

It is evidently a part of the Homily of Basil on the
words πρόσεχε σεαυτῷ (Migne, *Patr. Gr.* 31, col. 213).

19

Ἀπόσπασμα ψεστῶν Εὐαγγελίων κατ᾽ ἀναγνώσεις ἐν
μέρει ὑπεργεγραμμένον μετὰ συντόμων σημειώσεων περὶ τοῦ

Ἁγίου Παντελεήμωνος καὶ τοῦ Ἁγίου Καλλινικίου. λα΄ × κγ΄. δίστηλον.

Fragment of an erased lectionary, partly written over with short notices of St Panteleeimon and St Kallinikos. 31 cm. × 23 ; two columns.

20

Ἐρείπια χειρογράφου ἐν χονδροῖς κεφαλαιώδεσι γράμμασι, μέρος ἀκολουθίας τινός. τεμάχια ἑπτὰ ἢ ὀκτώ.

Remains of a book in rude uncials, a part of an akolouthia. Seven or eight pieces.

21

Ἁπλοῦν φύλλον παλίμψηστον· τὸ ἓν μέρος ἀναγεγραμμένον μετὰ τῆς ἀρχῆς τῆς πρὸς Ῥωμαίους Ἐπιστολῆς συριστί. τὸ ὑποκείμενόν ἐστι ἀπὸ Ἀριθμῶν λβ΄ κθ΄—λ΄. τοῦ ἑβδόμου αἰῶνος.

Single palimpsest leaf re-written on one side with the beginning of the Epistle to the Romans. The underwriting is from Numbers xxxii. 29—30; seventh century[1].

22

Ἀπόσπασμα τοῦ Εὐαγγελίου Ἰωάννου (κεφ. κα΄) ἀπὸ συναξαρίου τινός. κθ΄ × κα΄. τοῦ ἐννάτου αἰῶνος.

Fragment of the Gospel of John (c. xxi.) from a lectionary. 29 × 21 ; ninth century.

23

Ἀπόσπασμα ὁμιλίας ἐν πλαγίοις κεφαλαιώδεσι γράμμασιν. κϛ΄ × ιθ΄. δίστηλον· τοῦ ἐννάτου αἰῶνος.

Fragment of a homily in two columns: in sloping uncials of the ninth century. 26 cm. × 19.

[1] This is *Sinai Fragments*, No. 1.

24 25

Δύο τεμάχια ἀραβικοῦ βιβλίου ὑφ᾽ ὅ ἐστιν ἑλληνικὸν
παλίμψηστον ἀσκητικῆς διατριβῆς· φύλλα κδ᾽ καὶ λα᾽.

Two portions of an Arabic book, underneath which is a
Greek palimpsest of an ascetic treatise. 24 and 31 leaves
respectively.

The rubrics are still legible in certain places; e.g.

τοῦ αγτοῦ περὶ ἀκτημοσύνης ἐν ᾧ καὶ περὶ φιλαργυρίας

and the text is not difficult to decipher.

I subjoin a specimen :

ποίοις βρώμασιν ἑορτάσει· ὁ
δὲ θεόδουλος ἐν ποίοις χαρίσ-
μασιν πλουτήσει·
Ξένου ἐπιδημήσαντος εἰς ἀγά-
πην· ὅλος ἐκ γαστριμαργίας
κινεῖται· καὶ παράκλησιν ἀδελ-
φοῦ τὴν ἑαυτοῦ κατάλυσιν
λογίζεται κτέ.

It is an extract from the Scala Paradisi (Grad. xiv).

26

Ἀπόσπασμα τροπαρίου.
Fragment of a troparion.

27

Δύο φύλλα τροπαρίου.
Double leaf of a troparion.

28

Ἀπόσπασμα ἑλληνικοῦ χειρογράφου ἐν κεφαλαιώδεσι
γράμμασι τοῦ ἐννάτου αἰῶνος.

Fragment of a Greek book in ninth century uncials.

Ἀπόσπασμα τοῦ βίου τοῦ Ἁγίου Σαβᾶ.

It is a portion of the life of St Saba and apparently

belongs to the same MS. as the fragment numbered 17, as
may be inferred from the following transcript:

ἁΓίΟΥ ⲠⲚⳞ ⲤΥΝⲉⲣΓίΑ.
ἐΝ Δⲉ Τῶ Μέⲥω ΤΟῦ ⳨ⲉΙΜΆⲣ
ⲣΟΥ . ΜΙΚⲣὸΝ ἐΓΚΤΗⲣΙΟΝ, ⳙ
ΚΟΔόΜΗⳞⲉΝ . ἐΝ ⳙ ἩΓΙΑⳞΜέΝⲟ̄.
ΚΑὶ ὅΤⲉ ΤΙΝὰ ⳉέΝΟΝ ⲠΑⲣΑ
ⲂΑλλΟΝΤΑ ἐΔⲉ⳨ⲉΤΟ . ⳨ⲉΙⲣΟ
ΤΟΝΙΑΝ ἔ⳨ΟΝΤΑ ⲠⲣⲉⳞⲂΥΤ
ⲣΟΥ . ἐⲠΟίⲉΙ ἀΥΤΟΝ ἐΚΤⲉ
λⲉῖΝ ⲉΝ Τῶ ⲉΓΚΤΗⲣίω
ΤΗΝ ἀΝΑⳝΟⲣΆΝ

29

Ἀπόσπασμα ἑλληνικοῦ χειρογράφου ἐν κεφαλαιώδεσι
γράμμασιν. τοῦ ἐννάτου αἰῶνος.

Fragment of a ninth century Greek uncial: e.g.

. . . . ἀΥΤΟῖⳞ ἐΑΝ ΜⲉίΝωⳞΙΝ ωⳞ ΚΑ
θⲱⳞ ⳝΗⳞΙΝ ὁ ΑⲠΟⳞΤΟλΟⳞ . ⲉἰ Δⲉ ὀΥΚ
ἐΓΚⲣΑΤⲉΥΟΝΤΑΙ . ΓΑΜΗⳞΆΤωⳞⲁ̄.
ΚⲣⲉΙΤΤΟΝ ΓΆⲣ ἐⳞΤΙΝ ΓΑΜΉⳞΑΙ ἤ
ⲠΥⲣΟῦⳞθΑΙ· ΤΑ Δⲉ λΟΙⲠἀ ⲠΑΝΤΑ
ἀⳝΟⲣΙⳌⲉⳞθω ΜΑΚⲣΆΝ . ⲠΟⲣΝⲉίΑ . ΜΟΙ
⳨ⲉΙΑ ΚΤέ.

30

Ἕξ φύλλα τροπαρίου ἐν χονδροῖς κεφαλαιώδεσι γράμμασι νεωτέρας ἐποχῆς.

Six leaves of a troparion in rude uncials of late date.

31

Ἀπόσπασμα ἐν κεφαλαιώδεσιν ἑλληνικοῖς γράμμασιν·
τοῦ δεκάτου αἰῶνος.

Fragment in Greek uncials; tenth century.

32

Ἀπόσπασμα ἐν ἑλληνικοῖς κεφαλαιώδεσι γράμμασι νεωτέρας ἐποχῆς.

Fragment in late Greek uncials.

33

Ἀπόσπασμα ἐν χονδροῖς πλαγίοις κεφαλαιώδεσι γράμμασιν.

Fragment in thick sloping uncials.

34

Ἀπόσπασμα διστήλου κειμένου σλαβικοῦ χειρογράφου.

Fragment of a bicolumnar text of a Slavonic (?) writer.

35

Δύο φύλλα τροπαρίου τινὸς συρραπτόμενα· ἐν φύλλον ἐν γραφῇ τὸ ἥμισυ κεφαλαιώδει, τὸ ἥμισυ τρεχούσῃ.

Two leaves sewn together of a troparion; one leaf in a hand which is half uncial, half cursive.

36

Μέρος φύλλου ἑλληνικοῦ χειρογράφου ἐν χονδροῖς πλαγίοις κεφαλαιώδεσι γράμμασιν.

Part of a leaf of Greek writing in coarse sloping uncials.

37

Ἀπόσπασμα συναξαρίου ἐν μικροῖς κεφαλαιώδεσι γράμμασι νεωτέρας ἐποχῆς.

Fragment of a lectionary in small late uncials.

38

Ἀπόσπασμα τροπαρίου ἐν χονδροῖς κεφαλαιώδεσι γράμμασιν.

Fragment of a troparion in coarse uncials.

39

Δύο φύλλα εὐχολογίου ἐν κεφαλαιώδεσι γράμμασι τοῦ ἐννάτου ἢ τοῦ δεκάτου αἰῶνος.

Two leaves of an euchology in ninth or tenth century uncials.

40

Ἓν φύλλον εὐχολογίου ἐν κεφαλαιώδεσι γράμμασι νεωτέρας ἐποχῆς.

Leaf of an euchology in late uncials.

41

Ἀπόσπασμα τῶν Πράξεων τῶν Ἀποστόλων ἐν κεφαλαιώδεσι γράμμασι τοῦ δεκάτου αἰῶνος.

Fragment of the Acts of the Apostles in uncials of the tenth century.

42

Ὀκτὼ φύλλα παλιμψήστου χειρογράφου εὐχολογίου ἐν κεφαλαιώδεσι γράμμασι τοῦ ὀγδόου αἰῶνος.

Eight leaves of a palimpsest book of prayers in uncials of the eighth or ninth century.

43

Δύο φύλλα τροπαρίου ἐν ἑλληνικοῖς τρέχουσι γράμμασιν.

Two leaves of a troparion in Greek cursive.

44

Ἀποσπάσματα δύο φύλλων ἐν κεφαλαιώδεσι γράμμασι τοῦ ἐννάτου ἢ τοῦ δεκάτου αἰῶνος.

Fragments of a double leaf of uncial writing of the ninth or tenth century.

45

Ἓν φύλλον ἐν τρέχουσι γράμμασι παρέχον μέρος λειτουργίας.

Leaf of a cursive writing containing some liturgical matter.

46

Τεμάχιον φύλλου ἐν κεφαλαιώδεσι γράμμασι νεωτέρας ἐποχῆς.

Part of a leaf of late uncial writing.

47

Δύο μικρὰ φύλλα περιέχοντα φράσεις ἑλληνικάς τινας ἐν λατινικοῖς γράμμασιν.

Small double leaf containing some transliterated Greek sentences in Latin letters.

48

'Απόσπασμα φύλλου ἐν χονδροῖς κεφαλαιώδεσι γράμμασι νεωτέρας ἐποχῆς.

Fragment of a leaf in very coarse late uncials.

49

'Αποσπάσματα δύο φύλλων τροπαρίου ἐν ἀρχαίοις τρέχουσι γράμμασιν.

Fragments in an early cursive from a troparion, two leaves.

50

Τὸ ἰβηρικὸν Ψαλτήριον ἐπὶ παπύρου· ἔχει πολλὰ φύλλα.

An Iberian Psalter (?) on papyrus; very many leaves.

51

'Απόσπασμα φύλλου ἐν χονδροῖς κεφαλαιώδεσι γράμμασιν.

Fragment of a leaf in rude uncials.

52

Τεμάχια δύο φύλλων ψεστῆς ἑλληνικῆς γραφῆς τοῦ ἐννάτου αἰῶνος.

Part of a double leaf of erased Greek writing of the ninth century.

53

Τρία φύλλα παλίμψηστα εἰς ἒξ τετυλιγμένα.

Three palimpsest leaves which have been folded into six.

54

Προσθέτω δύο σελίδας ἐν συριακῇ τῆς Παλαιστίνης τῷ δεσίμῳ τοῦ ἰβηρικοῦ χειρογράφου ἀριθ. λβ΄ συγκεκολλημένας.

I add here two pages of Palestinian Syriac which are pasted in the cover of the Iberian MS. *Cod. Sin. Iber. 32.*

Fol. 1 recto.

Col. *b*	Col. *a*
Matt. xiv. 9—13.	Matt. xiv. 5—9.

ܒܡܢܝܢܬܐ ܘܗܘܐ
ܠܗܪܘܕܝܣ: ܠܡ
ܒܡܘܡܐ ܐܘܕܝ
ܠܗ̇ ܕܢܬܠ ܠܗ
ܡܢܐ ܕܬܫܘܠ
... ܗܘ ܕܝ
ܕܗܘܬ ܐܠܝܦܐ
ܥܡ ܐܢܫܗ
ܐܡܪܐ ܗܒ
ܠܝ ܗܒܝܐ ܥܠ
ܕܗܥܘܥܐ

ܘܐܬܝܗܒ
ܠܬܠܬܐ ܘܐܢܬ...
ܝܬܗ ܠܐܝܟܠܗ
ܘܩܪܒܘ
ܬܠܡܝܕܘܗܝ
ܐܪܝܡܘ ܒܩܠ⌜ܪ⌝ܐ
ܘܩܒܪܘ ܝܬܗ.
ܘܐܬܘ ܐܡܪܘ
ܠܡܪܐ ܝܫܘܥ
ܟܕ ܕܝ ܫܡܥ
ܡܪܐ ܝܫܘܥ

Fol. 2 recto

Col. *a*

John ii. 23—iii. 1

ܕܒܥܐܕܐ ܦܨܚ
ܗܝܡܢܘ ܒܫܡܗ
ܣܓܝܐܢ ܐܬܘܬܐ
ܕܗܘܐ ܥܒܕ
ܗܘ ܕܝ ܡܪܐ
ܝܫܘܥ ܠܐ
ܗܘܐ ܡܗܝܡܢ
ܕܝܡܗ ܠܗܘܢ
ܠܟܠ ܕܗܘܐ
ܗܘ ܡܒܪ ܒܘܠ
ܫܕܐ ܘܕܠܐ ܗܘܐ
ܥܪܝܢ ܕܢܣܗܕ

Col. *b*

John iii. 2—

. . . .
. . . .
ܐܢܫ . . . . . .
ܥܠ ܕ . . . . . .
ܐܬܝܐ . . . . .
ܕܐܬ . . . .
ܐܢ ܗܘܐ ܐܠܗܐ
ܥܡܗ ܐܦܢܝ
ܡܪܐ ܝܫܘܥ
ܘܐܡܪ ܠܗ ܐܡܝܢ
ܐܡܪܢܐ ܠܟ ܕܐ...
ܠܐ ܡܬܠܕ...

55

Δύο φύλλα ἐν συριακῇ τῆς Παλαιστίνης, ἐν τῷ δεσίμῳ
τοῦ συριακοῦ χειρογράφου ἀριθ. η´ εὑρηθέντα.

Two leaves in Palestinian Syriac, found in the cover of
the Syriac MS. No. 8. They appear to be fragments of
a hymn in honour of the Apostles Peter and Paul.

I.

Καὶ ἀπὸ τῆς προηγουμένης σελίδος·

II.

Καὶ ἀπὸ τῆς ἐπομένης σελίδος·

....
....
....
....
....

....
....
....
....
.... ܠܩܘܠܝ ܕܐ
.... ܕܓܠܝܘܬܐ ܡܢ
.... ܐ ܣܘܦܩ̈ܐ
.... ܐܝܪ ܠܩܘܠܩ
.... ܘܗܪܝܙܐ
.... ܠܘܐ ܡܢ
..........................ܣܘܦܩ̈ܐ
..........................ܟܒܒܒܪܐ
.... ܒܚܠܣܪ
.... ܠܒܐܬܘܗ

APPENDIX. No. II.

The following additional notes have been kindly sent to me by Mr John F. Stenning, after his return from Mount Sinai in April of this year.

No. 2.

The first 10 ff. are from a Synaxarion, late, beginning at Matt. v. 29 b—the MS. proper begins at f. 11 = Matt. xiii. 42.

ff. 17—40 another insertion from a late MS.

f. 40 = Mark ix. 5 b. The original MS. reappears and continues down to John v. 1.

Seq. 6 leaves from a Synaxarion—palimpsest. (I have identified 3 pages of the palimpsest with Mark xiii. 10—31; xi. 28 b—xii. 14 and xv. 32—xvi. 6—they all agree with the Peshitto.)

Seq. John vii. 50—xix. 12 in the original MS.

Seq. 4 ff. on paper, completing S. John.

Seq. 14 ff. of a Synaxarion on vellum—palimpsest. Passages identified are f. 1 = Luke iv. 41 b—v. 13; ff. 8—14 = Luke i. 54—ii. 2; vii. 40—viii. 8; iv. 23—41 a; iv. 2—23; vi. 34—49; John xv. 5 b—xiv. 7 b—27 a.

Seq. Synaxarion on paper.

No. 3.

Defective at the beginning—originally restored on paper which has been torn out.

MS. begins at Romans ii. 6 but the first 2 folios are very defective.

Date. 7th century.

No. 4.

At the end is a page of Arabic containing the 4th chapter of Basilius on monastic life.

No. 5.

The MS. begins at Romans xi. 22 b; 4 ff. restored. Those beginning at 1 Cor. vii. 36 and 1 Cor. xi. 17 are palimpsest—taken apparently from a homily on the Psalms.

Epistle to the Hebrews defective at the end—the last words are x. 28 ܥܠ ܦܘܩ ܕܬܪ

Seq. The Acts of the Apostles—James—1 Peter (after i. 2 a fresh section commences under the heading

(.ܐܓܪܬܐ ܕܦܛܪܘܣ ܘܝܥܩܘܒ.

Seq. 1 John i. 1—3 b.

Seq. (By a different hand.) 2 Peter, 1 John, 2 John, 3 John, Jude.

No. 6.

Date 1178 A.D.—many leaves are palimpsest but the under writing is not early.

At the end are 2 ff. containing stories about Greek philosophers numbered 25—37. At the top of the second folio is a heading ܩܠ ܡܬܐ ܐܝܢܝܐ ܕܦܠܝܣܘܦܐ ܐܠܦܘܠܝ.

No. 8.

Date must be later than the 8th century—more probably it belongs to the 10th.

The first half consists of selections from Genesis, Proverbs and Isaiah in regular rotation—in the latter half are sections from the other books of the O. T. and also from the N. T. including parts of 1 John and 1 Peter, which vary from the ordinary text.

One section from Daniel contains the Prayer of Azariah and the Song of the Three.

No. 10.

Defective at the beginning.

The first part consists mainly of a series of doctrinal questions addressed to Julianists, Nestorians, Jacobites and other heretics by Mar Proba, Ambrose of Milan, Leontes (a monk of Palestine), Anastasius, John, etc.

Seq. Epiphanius—according to the title, a translation of names from Hebrew into Syriac—a small section.

Seq. A brief history ܐܒܘܢ The first part simply a reckoning of the years from Adam to the Flood etc. up to the time of our Lord according to the LXX. and then according to the numbering of the Syrians. The latter part gives a brief history from the time of our Lord to the Council of Constantinople under Justin.

Seq. Extracts from Jacob of Serug, John, Theophilus, John Chrysostom, Ephraem, Jacob, Proclus, Cyril.

Seq. Homilies with quotations from a number of the Fathers—an extract from the Apostolic Canons, on Priests—a confession of faith—extracts from Anastasius, Ephraem, Evagrius.

For notices at the end see the Catalogue.

No. 14.

Title. "A collection from holy writings for the benefit of souls."

ff. 1—23. Questions addressed to Macarius with his answers.

f. 24. A fragment of the life of the holy Nilus.

f. 27 b. Klimax.

f. 31. Another fragment.

f. 39. Klimax.

f. 47. Macarius.

f. 53. ܘܐܠܩܣܝ ܐܣܪ (? Cassianus περὶ ἐγκρατείας).

f. 57 b. John of ܩܪܦܬܝܐ ; cf. Greek MS. 461, where Ἰωάννης Καρπάθιος is mentioned.

f. 64 b. Isaac of Nineveh.

f. 93 b. Gregory, bishop of Nyssa (ܪܘܣܝܐ).

f. 95. Isaac.

ff. 112 b—118. Simeon and Isaiah.

f. 127 b. Sayings from the philosophers Plato, Didymus, Themistius.

f. 130 b. Letter of Gregory to Basilius—Cyril.

f. 131. Aristotle.

f. 140 b. Dionysius—sayings of Serapion, Theodorus, Ephraem, Cyril, Chrysostom (ܦܘܡܐ ܕܕܗܒܐ), Athanasius, Julius of Rome, Justin, Ephraem, etc.

The MS. consists of a number of fragments bound up together—some of which are considerably later than the 10th century.

No. 15.

Begins at Acts ii. 27, p. ܐ—single column.

p. ܠܗ James.

p. ܩܟ 1 Peter.

p. ﺳﻖ 2 Peter—by a different hand—much later—palimpsest.

[The palimpsest is in 2 columns—not later than the 6th century—and contains :—

		right column	left column
p. ܩܝܐ		Lev. xxiii. 15 b—19 b	xxiii. 22 c—27 a
p. „ b		xxii. 30 b—xxiii. 2	xxiii. 8—12
p. ܩܝܒ		ix. 21—24 a	x. 3 b—5
p. „ b		x. 9 b—12 b	x. 15 b—17 b
p. ܩܝܓ		x. 6—9 a	x. 12 b—15 b
p. „ b		ix. 15—20 a	ix. 24 a—x. 3 a
p. ܩܝܕ		xxiii. 2 b—7 b	xxiii. 13—15 b
p. „ b		xxiii. 20—22	xxiii. 27 b—31
p. ܩܝܗ		xxi. 9 b—12 b	xxi. 18 b—
p. „ b		xx. 20—23 b	xx. 27—xxi. 5 a
p. ܩܟܐ (v. infra)		xix. 19 b—22	xix. 27 c—32
p. „ b		xix. 36—xx. 2 a	xx. 6 b—11 b]

p. ܩܟܚ 1 John—by the same hand as the Acts.

p. ܩܟܐ = 1 John iv. 1. 6 folios by the same hand as 1 Peter—palimpsest, but the under writing is in most cases completely obliterated.

p. ܩܣܘ Ep. to the Romans—2 columns—some leaves restored.

p. ܪܣܚ (Ep. to the Hebrews) 17 palimpsest leaves—single column—a later insertion.

p. ܪܠ End of Ep. to the Hebrews. 2 columns.

Seq. An explanation of the headings and rubrics—late.

Seq. A Synaxarion—very late.

No. 16.

(1) The beginning of this section must now be missing, if the enumeration of the folios is correct. The numbering of the folios should now be

(1) fol. 1—50. (2) fol. 51—56. (3) fol. 56—69.
(4) fol. 69—76. (5) fol. 76—85. (6) fol. 85—90.
(7) fol. 90—96. (8) fol. 96—104. (9) fol. 104—107.
(10) fol. 107—109. [(Discourse of Theano.) (11) fol. 109—115. (12) fol. 115—178. (13) fol. 178 ad finem.]

After the commentaries of Chrysostom follow (1) a genealogy of the Virgin Mary and of Joseph; (2) Discourses of Jacob of Edessa, Ephraem, John and Jacob, on Paradise.

No. 20.

Date 6527 of the world, i.e. 1019 A.D.
At the end is a Synaxarion.

No. 27.

The Syriac palimpsest is written in a fine regular Estrangelo hand of the 6th or 7th century.

ff. 3 b & 8 = Num. xxvii. 16 b—-xxviii. 11 b.
ff. 4 b & 7 = Lev. i. 17—iii. 1.
ff. 5 b & 6 = „ xix. 22—xx. 4.
f. 9 = „ xiii. 25 b—28 b & 32 b—36 a.
ff. 10 b & 17 = Exod. xxxiv. 27 ff.
ff. 12 b & 15 = „ ix. 7—22.
ff. 13 b & 14 = „ xxxix. end—xl. 15.
ff. 19 b & 22 = Genesis xlvi.
ff. 20 b & 21 = „ xli. 33—43 & 43—52.
f. 25 = Num. vii. 60 ff.

Towards the end Dt. xxix. 10—xxxi. 1, is easily read on another palimpsest leaf—the other leaves are illegible.

No. 28.

Quarto—single columns.

Inc.   I. Kings vi. 16 ܪܒܚܕ.

Exp.   II. Kings xi. 3 ܘܚܕܠܐ ܐܒܪܬܕ ܠܐ ܐܪܝܣܐ.

No. 31.

Small regular hand of the 10th century.

Homilies of Mar Isaiah (or Mar Isaac?), Mar Ephraem.

Seq.   An account of various Egyptian solitaries who were tempted by Satan.

Seq.   Stories of Egyptian Fathers taken from the account given by Palladius the bishop.

Seq.   Homilies of Mar John the solitary and Mar Jacob.

No. 33.

The homilies of Mar Isaiah—apparently agreeing in order and substance with No. 26. The MS. does not go beyond the homily ܠܒܠܬ ܐܠ ܐܒܪܝܣܕܪ.

It is written in an irregular Estrangelo hand of the 11th century—possibly later—some leaves are palimpsest, the under writing being part of a book of homilies.

No. 35.

ff. 1—7 are early—they contain I. Sam. i. 1—iii. 6 (with a lacuna of ch. i. 4 b—25).

Then follows by a later hand :—II. Sam. xxiii. 10—xxiv. 20.

After another lacuna the MS. proceeds with II. Sam. xx. 22 b (ch. xxi. 7—16 wanting)—xxii. 26.

A fresh section then commences with I. Sam. iv. 2.

The MS. is clearly composed of two, if not three, fragments, of which the first is very early, viz. I. Sam. i. 1 —iii. 6.

Probably there was originally another leaf, containing iii. 7—iv. 1 bound up in this MS.—and to this section was added the later one beginning at iv. 2.

The third fragment inserted between these two sections, viz. that containing II. Sam. xxiii. 10—xxiv. 20 and II. Sam. xx. 22 b—xxii. 26—is also later than the first section—the writing resembling that of the section, I. Sam. iv. 2—end.

No. 36.

Some leaves palimpsest—the under writing in a small regular hand—in double columns—apparently a book of homilies. The palimpsest writing is very like that of MS. 39.

No. 46.

I should ascribe to the 8th century.

No. 52.

Hardly so early as the 7th century—it must be at least a century later.

No. 56.

Read "and supplemented by homilies of Mar Isaac, Mar Jacob and Anastasius of Antioch."

No. 59.

The homilies are numbered 63—75.

Cambridge:

PRINTED BY C. J. CLAY, M.A. AND SONS,

AT THE UNIVERSITY PRESS.

www.ingramcontent.com/pod-product-compliance
Ingram Content Group UK Ltd.
Pitfield, Milton Keynes, MK11 3LW, UK
UKHW012021280225
455719UK00011B/428